restoring

JOY

DEBORAH FINN

Restoring Joy, acrylic on canvas, 20" x 40"

"Working with acrylics and the palette knife, my self-taught path has allowed my true artistic voice to emerge — a journey that I believe is never-ending." – *Deborah Finn, artist*

Deborah Finn lives and works in Hamilton, Ontario.

Illustrations by Caillin Kowalczyk

ISBN: 979-8-218-64603-5
1st printing 2025

restoring

JOY

FORTY DAYS & FORTY NIGHTS
ON THE CAMINO DE SANTIAGO

by

COLLEEN O'TOOLE

STONE BOAT EDITIONS

Dedicated to my daughter

And a heartfelt thank you to all the beautiful souls
who walked the path with me, including the spirits.

PRAISE FOR *RESTORING JOY*

DAVID RAMSAY, editor (*Pilgrim Footprints*) and retired journalist:

Restoring Joy was truly a great read. I was hooked from page one, loved the sweet and hopeful ending, and enjoyed everything in between.

Here's my strange way of knowing if a book—fiction or nonfiction—is one I find exceptional. Rarely does it happen with nonfiction, which usually requires a more concentrated effort from me.

I not only read the words, but in books I really love, the words play out in my mind much like a great film might. So I quickly go from reading the words to subconsciously translating them into images in my brain and forget that I'm actually reading. The pages just turn themselves. *Restoring Joy* did that for me.

JOE CURRO, National Pilgrimage Association leader:

This is a deeply spiritual book. It is punctuated throughout with observations and epigraphs from a wide array of faith and wisdom traditions, including large helpings of Buddhist teachings... and... humor abounds.

This book itself is magical, hopeful, uplifting, and well worth the read.

DENNIS GARNHUM, Author of *Toward Beauty* & theatre director:

It's delicious, delicate, and thoughtful writing.

A true honour to walk with Colleen in this deeply honest book. I held my breath many times—wanting her to find the inspiration that the Camino can provide. And when it does arrive, it made me grin from ear to ear.

A distinct, beautiful voice.

DR. STEPHEN F. HALLER, professor, Pilgrimage Studies:

Colleen O'Toole's story of her pilgrimage manages to combine a captivating story of humorous events while sharing a personal journey of inner transformation and healing which readers will recognize and find absorbing. I found myself laughing many times at her deadpan delivery of an absurd comment that often follows a serious remark about an inner struggle. It is a good read that will leave you feeling hopeful.

JENNIFER COPELAND, MN RN Counsellor (OAMHP):

This heartfelt book is a gift for mothers experiencing the pain and powerlessness of alienation.

With humour and vulnerability, Colleen shares her journey through trauma and the reclaiming of her right to live and find joy. Her story is an embodiment of the faith, trust, and courage that's needed to live with grief and loss, and speaks to the possibility of the love and joy that's available alongside it. A beautiful read!

ROSALIND BRACKENBURY, Writer, Poet, Pilgrim:

I wanted to be with her every step of the way. She's great company, even in wild weather, with sore feet, living through sleepless nights with snoring companions...Transparent honesty, astonished delight, and a rare pleasure.

I loved this book.

DAN MULLINS, Musician, Podcaster, Pilgrim:

I loved every page!

FORTY DAYS & FORTY NIGHTS

ON THE CAMINO DE SANTIAGO

CONTENTS

CONTENTS

The Meseta

Galicia

Santiago de Compostela

San Nicolas

Poblacion

Carrion de los Condes

Terradillos de los Templarios

Bercianos

Leon Catedral

Rabanal

O Cebreiro

Filloval

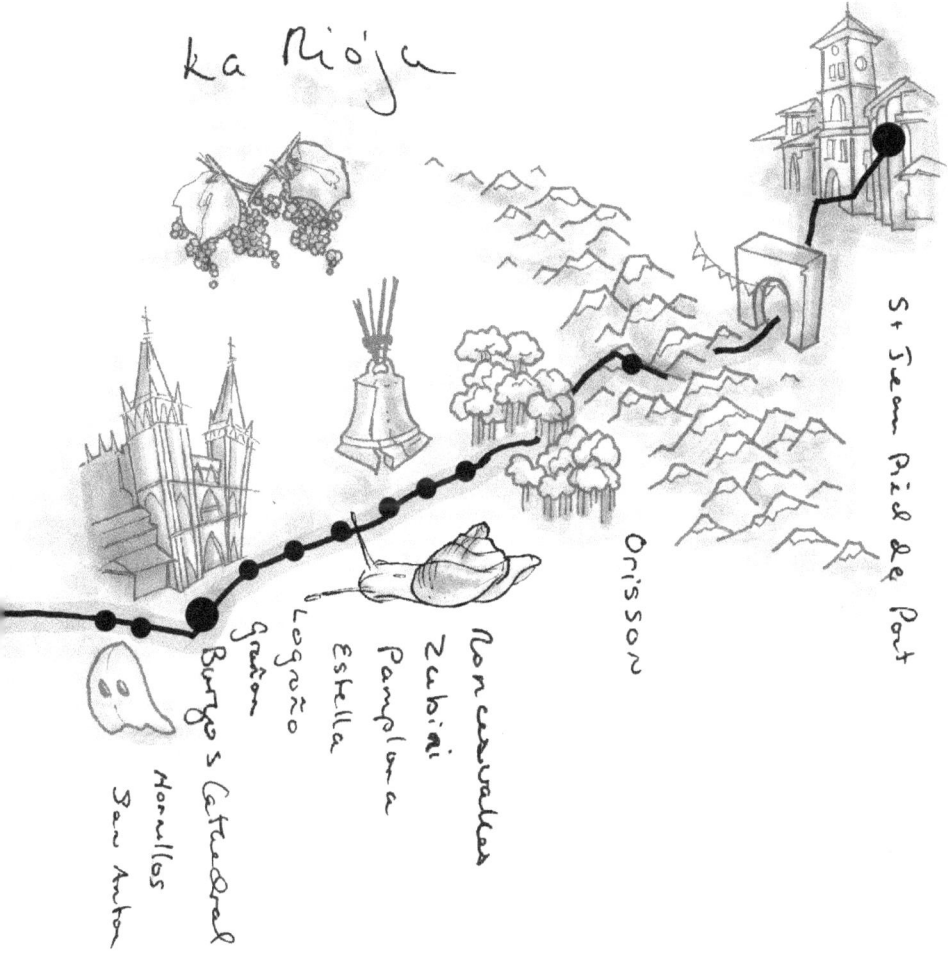

La Rioja

St Jean Pied de Port

Orisson

Roncesvalles
Zubiri
Pamplona
Estella
Logroño
Grañon
Burgos Cathedral
Hornillos
San Anton

GLOSSARY

THE CAMINO – *El Camino de Santiago*, The Way of Saint James in English, or simply, The Way.

ALBERGUE – A pilgrim hostel, often run by volunteers, municipalities, or religious organizations. Accommodations are usually dorm-style, budget-friendly, with common areas like a kitchen.

BASQUE REGION – Culturally distinct region of Spain that is contiguous with *le pays basque français* in southwest France. A pilgrim walking on the Camino Francés (the French Route of the Camino de Santiago) from the French side of the Pyrenees starts in Basque Country.

BOCADILLO – Sandwich made with a small bun or small baguette; common fare in bars and cafés along the Camino.

BOTAFUMEIRO – A giant incense burner used during special Pilgrim Masses in Santiago de Compostela Cathedral. It swings dramatically across the transept.

BUEN CAMINO – Traditional greeting amongst and to pilgrims meaning "good way."

CAFÉ CON LECHE – Literally, "coffee with milk," a morning favorite of pilgrims.

COMMUNITAS – A deep sense of shared experience, connection, and equality among people going through a common journey or transformative event, where usual social hierarchies fade.

COMPOSTELA – Document that can be earned by walking a minimum distance on the Camino to Santiago de Compostela for religious or spiritual reasons.

CREDENCIAL / CREDENCIALES (pl.) – Also known as the pilgrim's passport, this is a small folding booklet which proves someone is a pilgrim and therefore eligible to stay in pilgrim albergues (hostels). Pilgrims collect stamps in their credenciales to show where and when they stayed.

DONATIVO – Describes a special type of albergue that does not have a fee for overnight stay but requests a "responsible contribution" from pilgrims. Usually dormitory accommodation, sometimes offering a communal evening meal and, most importantly, offering a traditional Camino welcome similar to what would have been offered to pilgrims over centuries, who had little, but needed food, shelter, and safety for a night. Can also mean anything offered for which a donation is given, or the donation itself.

ENSALADA RUSA – A type of potato salad, ubiquitous along the Camino, and one of few menu offerings that suit vegetarians in a country where the cuisine heavily favors those eating fish and meat.

ETAPA – A stage or day's walk on the Camino. Pilgrims often plan their journeys by etapas, with each representing a segment between towns.

GALICIA – Celtic land within Spain in the northwest which includes the cathedral city of Santiago de Compostela.

GÎTE – *(French)* A guest house; alternative term for hostel, auberge, or albergue.

HOSPITALERO / HOSPITALERA – A volunteer or staff member who manages an albergue and offers hospitality to pilgrims.

LA RIOJA – Renowned wine region of La Rioja, west of the Pyrenees.

MESETA – A well-known, very flat, high plateau in Spain with vast open spaces. Taking about 7–8 days to walk, some find it challenging due to its monotony, while others regard it as the perfect meditative space.

MOCHILA – Spanish word for backpack. Pilgrims carry their belongings in a *mochila,* often keeping it as light as possible.

MUNICIPAL – Albergue run by the local municipality; inexpensive communal accommodation.

PARROQUIAL – Albergue run by the church; inexpensive communal accommodation for pilgrims, often donativo as well.

PEREGRINO / PEREGRINA – Spanish for pilgrim.

PILGRIM – Someone who is traveling for a religious or spiritual reason or who experiences a religious or spiritual insight along The Way.

REFUGIO – Literally, a refuge; the name historically given to rustic shelters along the Camino.

SCALLOP SHELL – The traditional symbol of the pilgrimage to Santiago, usually attached to backpacks; ancient pilgrims returned home with them from coastal Galicia.

SELLO – A stamp placed in your credencial at albergues, churches, bars, and other stops along the Camino. You'll need at least two per day in the final 100 km to receive the *Compostela*.

ULTREIA Y SUSEIA – Originally a medieval expression meaning "let's go further" and "let's go higher"; an original greeting between pilgrims with one saying the first part and the other replying with the second. Replaced these days by the pilgrim greeting, *Buen Camino!*.

WAYMARK / YELLOW ARROW – The ubiquitous yellow arrows that guide pilgrims along the route, often painted on walls, roads, rocks, and signposts.

PROLOGUE

Many people choose to walk the ancient pilgrimage, the 790-kilometer Camino de Santiago, for spiritual reasons, to get closer to God or their Faith. Others walk with an interest in history or culture. A whole bunch go after experiencing a break-up—whether from a relationship, a job, or a way of life— seeking a new direction or a deeper understanding of who they truly are.

Me? I wanted to die.

Most of me wanted to die anyway, and it turns out that distinction makes a big difference. I was teetering on the edge of the abyss and no one knew it. Thankfully, there existed a small, but persistent part of me, trying to convince the rest of me that there were reasons to stay alive—this was a big job, as there truly were no observable reasons, not observable to me anyway. And that same small but persistent part of me clawed my way back from the edge, packed my bag, pushed past opposition and injury and made my way to Spain.

Why the distress?

Fair to ask, but before we get too far down that road, I need to acknowledge that I didn't plan to begin this way.

I tried to leave out the part about wanting to die, the reasons why and just weave a hint of it into the story that follows. It seemed abrupt to launch right into despair. But in the end, it felt wrong, like I was keeping something back. You can always feel that. So, I am flouting storytelling wisdom and laying it bare on page one. It seemed especially important to be straightforward as the ties that bound me were hidden for a long time. I've waited many years and it is time to bring it into the light.

So, why the distress?

The short story is, too much grief for too long and no Joy. None. Zippo.

Joy seems extra, like a bonus, until it disappears. That is when we realize how essential it is. Joy and sorrow are close companions. You can't have one without the other. I didn't even remember what Joy looked like; didn't think I had any capacity for it. And life didn't seem worth bothering if there were to never be any Joy at all.

So, like a woman with her hair on fire looks for a bucket of water, I went looking for Joy.

As often happens when we set out on these journeys, I was thrown some obstacles before even beginning—the Universe testing to see if we really want the medicine. My biggest one, aside from general fear, came in the form of an undiagnosable foot injury which halted my training. I was advised to postpone the walk, but my advisers didn't know my foot was the least of my problems.

Wanting to die isn't something we talk about, unfortunately.

A month before leaving, I woke up, as usual, at three a.m., rubbing my sore, swollen foot, wondering about the impact it would have on my pilgrimage. That is the dangerous time, when everyone is asleep and your mind travels. Wondering was replaced with worry, then grief and finally fear. That's when I realized it wasn't about the foot. I was afraid that this walk would change nothing. That I could drag myself clear across Spain and still return to a life not worth living. Terrifying. Because this was my Hail Mary pass, as it were. I was out of ideas.

Familial alienation. Happens more than you'd think and is more devastating than you'd imagine. Once you've experienced it, you start to listen to people in a different way. You hear it in the pauses, see it in the facial expressions, find it in what is left unsaid. People don't talk about this because it is an experience full of shame, pain and blame.

There is always the well-meaning person who says, "Are you sure you aren't imagining it?" Yes, I've double checked that.

Even paid a small fortune for the expert therapist who said, with heart-breaking compassion, "I'm sorry, but there is nothing you can do now but keep the door open. It's going to be a while."

He paused while I absorbed this, then added, "And I have to tell you, they don't always come back—sometimes the damage is too great."

It was like being hit by a bus.

"I can't," I said, in shock. "I'll never make it."

"You need to take care of yourself in the meantime," he said.

For what, I wondered. Why bother?

Friends and family ask, "Did you try email? How about a letter?" Yes. I've tried it all. That is what keeps alienated parents hooked.

"Maybe there is another way, another book, another expert..." we say every time we pick ourselves up off the ground.

"But it's your child. You can't give up," they say.

No. We can't. We won't. We try to hold water in our hands and the grief goes on and on and on. That is not how grief is meant to work.

We hold the door open, but it is heavy. And they don't come. Some days, it is too much. You want to go to sleep and stay asleep. Some days the only reason you get up is because the dog needs to go out. (Luckily, I was left with a dog—Libby, a devoted beagle.)

It can't last forever, this static sorrow. Grief is meant to move. When it doesn't move, it makes you sick. Joy stops coming around because the dance doesn't make sense anymore, the steps all wrong and after a few years of that, well.

Why am I sharing all this?

Because someone needs to. It is happening much more than we know. I met many of the wounded on the Camino, both alienated parents and alienated adult children, which is partly why I decided to share this. We need to know we are not alone—especially with the kind of sorrow that no one can see.

I decided to write a blog while I made my pilgrimage from Saint-Jean-Pied-de-Port in France to Santiago de Compostela in the northwest corner of Spain, hoping my story might help shed some light on living with trauma and how the silence that often co-exists will steal your voice. It certainly stole my voice.

Back in 2016, when I finally understood what had been happening and in 2019 when I had very specific ideas of what I would do to make the pain stop, I didn't think I'd make it. Recovery seemed an impossible dream.

But I did make it. It is possible. If you are at the edge of the abyss, scratch and claw your way back to land. Life is worth it.

Get messy and claw until your fingers bleed, but don't give up. Talk to someone. There is more. There is light. Joy does not die, but sometimes, you do have to go looking for it.

Solvitur Ambulando, said Saint Augustine. It is solved by walking. And it may be a long old way, but it is worth it.

Keep going.

You cannot imagine what awaits you.

DEPARTURES,
PORTALS & THRESHOLDS
(Basque Country and La Rioja)

Departure
August 2019

"Sometimes any change is better than no change. Any action is often better than no action, especially if you have been stuck in an unhappy situation for a long time. If it is a mistake, at least you learn something. If you remain stuck, you learn nothing."
Eckhart Tolle

*And I'm off...*on a sweltering August afternoon at the Toronto Pearson airport, just me and my backpack, the latter weighing in at what I considered to be a reasonable fifteen pounds. Technically, if I had followed advice, it should have been two or three pounds lighter, but fifteen pounds is just three bags of sugar, right? Anyway, it was as light as I could get it and, believe me, I went through that bag and weighed everything with a kitchen scale including the underwear and the toothbrush options. It must be said, it bordered on the ridiculous.

I thought back to the Saturday morning my friend Lise watched with amusement at my kitchen table as I demonstrated, very seriously, the difference in weight between brand A dismal hiking undies and brand B even more dismal hiking undies, and the difference it made to lop off the end of a brush so you've got just the bristles. The passionate and slightly mad demonstration was enough to remind Lise why she was going to the all-inclusive in Cuba instead of the Camino.

Despite the pains taken to prepare myself for the journey, I was feeling (and looking), nervous, sweaty and doughy. Dim sum dumpling comes to mind. Within a day's travel, I would begin to discover if my interrupted preparation had been sufficient to carry me through the next 40 days and 40 nights of pilgrimage from the French side of the Pyrenees to Santiago de Compostela in Spain and finally to the sea, Muxía, if the fates allowed. And while I certainly wanted to get to Santiago and collect my Compostela, as that is the intended end of the pilgrimage, my heart's desire was to walk from the mountains until I saw the sun setting over the ocean and hopefully, bring myself back to life along the way. Santiago de Compostela, the destination for most, was simply a stop on the road for me and it had been an adventure already, just getting to the departure gate.

With rather messy inconvenience, I developed a mysterious pain and swelling in my foot sometime during preparing for the Camino, a condition which could be neither diagnosed nor treated effectively, and essentially laid me up for what should have been a month and a half of training before leaving for Spain. I had been walking every week in the spring with Dara and the dozen others that collected every morning on a fifteen to twenty kilometer walk through Toronto. They were nearly all pilgrims, people who had already completed the walk, and they were brimming with enthusiasm as well as tips and suggestions—great fun to be around—but I missed the whole summer because of my foot. It was suggested by some that I postpone the trip until the following spring, but, for me, that was impossible.

Many say that one is called to walk the Camino, something I felt in my bones and I felt that to not answer the call would be a mistake. Joseph Campbell, a master of mythological studies, wrote about the "refusal of the call" and from what I could tell, this does not turn out well. He talks about this refusal as an exit from the Hero's Journey of transformation into the Shadow Journey, where the undischarged energy becomes a toxin and we sabotage ourselves by reacting out of fear of the unknown. Resisting, bargaining and dragging one's feet are all quite natural, to be expected and found throughout our collective stories, but eventually, the call must be answered, or the situation deteriorates.

I did not need any more deterioration. Also, I felt the need for perspective that I hoped the Camino would provide, as all areas of my life were in paralysis. A midlife crisis, while distressing and confusing, points more toward an overall dissatisfaction with one's life, gnawing existential questions and a re-examining of life. I was indeed in midlife and unhappy was an understatement, but I was not having a midlife crisis.

To put it simply, I had become miserable—fixated and paralyzed by loss.

The issue was singular, though the fallout from the singular issue blanketed every area of my life. If that one point were resolved, I was certain life-force would return. Pinned by hope of a possible resolution (a resolution which was not in my power), for what seemed an interminable time, I fell into despair. That hopelessness grew to the extent that I found myself moving from passive suicidal ideation to something more active and persistent. Suicidal thoughts and risk exist along a continuum, ranging from passive thoughts of death to active suicidal urges, planning and intent. Levels of distress can vary and fluctuate over time, but the distress always needs attention. (See end of chapter for resources)

For several years, I had been wrestling with a profound grief and related impotence, trying to correct something that should have been fixable and yet was not. The loss gutted me. When we lose someone to death, we lose them once. Excruciatingly painful, without a doubt, yet if the pain is allowed to move, it can, over time, transform. When we lose a loved one to alienation, it is like a death that keeps on happening; one that we are not allowed to feel, that we get little to no support for, that is full of shame and often even blame.

When a mother is alienated from her child, she loses not only the child, but also in many ways, she loses motherhood. A whole life erased.

Eventually you can't remember what it was like; to be a mother who had a child.

Ambiguous loss. Disenfranchised grief. The loss happens repeatedly and, with the possibility of hope always on the distant horizon, one is hooked.

It has been impossible for me to walk away. How do you walk away from your daughter? I could think of nothing but what I had lost—my only child—and revising impotent strategies on how to correct it, the unavoidable fixation altering me, so much so that some part of me believed, and was getting more insistent by the day, that the only way to make this better was to die. Night after night I awoke, alone and terrified of my own mind. In short, I was not safe. My lack of preparation was the least of my problems.

Intractable sorrow and despair—that was my problem.

The history of the Camino de Santiago de Compostela is long and fascinating and could comprise an entire book itself, indeed, many already exist, so I will not offer an extensive elaboration here. In a nutshell, I planned to walk the 790-kilometer Camino Francés, which is one of several paths that traverse Europe, ending at the cathedral where the remains of St. James the Apostle are said to rest. People have been making the pilgrimage since at least the ninth century, being particularly popular in the Middle Ages. Not as risky as free-climbing, but not without hazard, as several memorials along the way attest.

The Camino Francés begins in Saint-Jean-Pied-de-Port in the French Pyrenees, wandering through Basque country to the city of Pamplona (a favorite haunt of Ernest Hemingway), passing through the vineyards of la Rioja to the beautiful city of Burgos. From there it crosses the high plateau of the Meseta, through León with its famous cathedral, drifting into the magical mists of Galicia, coming to completion for many at the cathedral in Santiago de Compostela, a small and bustling city. Some pilgrims continue the journey to the sea, to the town of Finisterre, the end of the earth.

Many make this pilgrimage for religious reasons and many others for deeply spiritual reasons not affiliated with any religion. There are pilgrims seeking to heal themselves from old wounds. People come who have sustained a great loss or have fought through an illness. Some come to offer thanks for all their blessings. Others come to scatter ashes. People come because they read a book or saw a movie and wanted a bit of the magic for themselves. Some people come to support a friend and don't discover why they are really there until much later. A constellation of deeply personal reasons, but once the decision is made to walk, the only relevant reason is one's own. I knew mine.

Not everyone takes forty days to complete the Francés route, many do it in a month and in fact the guidebooks that many pilgrims follow set out stages that anticipate one would complete the walk within thirty-three days. As I reviewed the distances outlined, I felt confident I could manage them, but I was not at all inclined to rush through and, moreover, had become attached to the idea of a forty-day journey. There are many lay references to forty days related to the time needed for purification, transformation and rebirth. Relevance is found in many religious traditions, for example in the biblical stories; there was the flood, Moses on the mountain, Lent and many more 40-day odysseys.

The purpose of my journey, a resurrection of spirit, felt in alignment with the historical significance of the number though perhaps not so grand, the result of this 40-day journey was, as you might imagine, of the utmost importance to me.

. . .

The airport was full of smiling travelers that late August afternoon, dragging along their colorful suitcases, heading

off in their attractive travel outfits. And then there was me—
sweating profusely in my earth-colored merino wool shirt, ugly
hiking pants and goofy shoes, wielding my bright backpack. I
didn't envy them, there was nowhere else I wanted to go but
to Spain, to an endless stretch of road, I just registered that
I looked different. I felt like I was floating just outside the
ordinary world, observing.

With a mix of excitement and fear, I trundled off into the
(mostly) unknown; me and my fifteen-pound pack. I had to
believe that anything, even abject failure, would be better than
the current state of things.

Anything.

Thoughts of suicide always need attention. Help lines are available 24/7.
Seek professional advice. If you or someone you know is experiencing thoughts
of self-harm or suicide, help is available. *You are not alone.*

- Crisis Services Canada (24/7 helpline): 1-833-456-4566
- Mental Health Crisis Line (Canada Wide): 1-888-893-8333
- Text Crisis Line (for those who prefer texting): 45645
- In the United States: Suicide & Crisis Lifeline – Dial 988 (Available 24/7,
confidential support). Crisis Text Line – Text HELLO to 741741 (24/7 support
via text).

For immediate, local support, please reach out to a healthcare professional or
visit your nearest emergency department. For additional resources, visit Crisis
Services Canada.

Please seek support if you are in crisis. Your well-being matters.

Toronto, Canada
to Saint-Jean-Pied-de-Port, France

A worrier by nature, or more likely by nurture, I did what I could to carefully plan my journey and avoid any avoidable travel miseries. And this may sound silly, but getting from your house to Saint-Jean-Pied-de-Port in time for dinner the next day is a major hurdle and is the subject of many a hot debate in online forums. To make my life easier, I decided to fly into Charles de Gaulle in Paris instead of Madrid since I was familiar with it and I wanted to be sure not to begin my journey by missing connections.

That is where I found myself on the following morning, after an uncomfortable, sleepless night in economy. Turns out I was familiar with this airport circa 1999 and guess what—it was not the same. Go figure. Brazenly optimistic to think I would remember an airport from two decades ago.

Thanks to the detours necessitated by the ongoing construction, I had to navigate French customs in *"franglais"* at least three times. How is that possible? Was I ever glad I didn't try to smuggle in the walking poles. I had intended to purchase a mobile plan for my phone in the airport, but in my circuitous route, I never did find the store. Although I believed I had a comfortable two and a half hours to do so, I just barely made the connector to Biarritz and threw myself onto the plane, a harried, squishy, dim sum dumpling, the last to board before they shut the doors. Yes, I was *that* person.

"Attention, Colleen O'Toole; s'il vous plaît, allez à la porte S3..."

A ride share to Saint-Jean-Pied-de-Port was waiting for me at the Biarritz airport when we landed, with a friendly guy, Jean, at the wheel. Jean, as it turned out, drove like a madman, even by my Boston standards. There were two women from Canada who were to share the ride with me, Ann and Donna. They were planning to walk the Camino together and had started by relaxing for a couple days by the beach in Biarritz.

Why didn't I think of that?

"That sounds like a nice way to begin," I said. "Did you enjoy it?"

"Oh yes, it was a wonderful couple of days," said Donna, looking lovely in a blue flowered sundress.

Beautiful, but it looked like cotton. I wondered if she weighed that.

"Maybe a bit too much red wine," laughed Ann.

They looked happy and confident, two friends in their mid-fifties, fresh from their beach holiday. At no point had I even considered walking with a friend, and though I knew the reasons that brought me here required some solitude that traveling with friends would not bring, I could see how sweet it might be and part of me longed for it. I knew two or three girlfriends who would be great company on this journey.

The driver, Jean, popped the trunk and put my little red Osprey backpack inside.

"How far do you plan to go?" asked Ann, sizing up my pack, one eyebrow raised.

"Santiago and hopefully Finisterre," I said as I watched Jean load up their suitcases and duffel bags—two each. My little pack looked lost in there and I started to feel like I had left something behind. Many, many somethings.

"Wow," said Donna, incredulous. "And that's all you have?"

"Mmhmm. But I'm two pounds over," I said, feeling lost and not at all sure of anything now. They didn't bother to ask what it was that I found myself two pounds over, or why on earth that might concern me, likely determining I was mad and moved on to chit chat.

They were doing a hotel, ship-your-bag style Camino and wished to have no part of the potential bedbugs and cacophony of snoring at the *albergues* (or hostels), perhaps not understanding that bedbugs do not discriminate.

Nevertheless, I imagined the contents of their bags with envy—hairbrushes without the handle lopped off, multiple pairs of underthings, ...a hairdryer.

Ah, self-doubt, I see you have arrived.

Oh dear, what have I done?

As their happy chitter chatter continued, I looked out the window as we whizzed past the tall pine trees, eventually seeing the mountains rising in the distance, trying to practice trust as Jean hugged the corners like he was running from the police. It was a beautiful ride through the countryside, but I was nervous and had no further recollection of what we talked about as I was fixated on thinking that I was ill-prepared and alone and truly had no idea where I was going or what I was doing.

When we were deposited outside their hotel, the driver gave me directions into the old part of town where I would find my hostel across from the pilgrim office. I immediately got lost. However, Saint-Jean-Pied-de-Port is a pretty little town, so it was not an unpleasant kind of lost and everyone knows the pilgrim office, so once I asked, I was found.

Lost and found on day zero.

I took this as a good sign.

The hostel was closed when I arrived, so I went to get a *credencial* (pilgrim passport) and a scallop shell (symbol of the pilgrim) for my backpack. The expanse of blank squares on the passport, which must be stamped each night, unnerved me yet again—there were so many days ahead. All those days would bring new challenges, the first one being that daunting climb straight up the mountain I had seen on the way in from the car window.

Could I possibly walk that far and meet all the challenges ahead with so little preparation?

Alone?

While I waited in line outside the office, I met a handful of friendly Canadians.

"Guessing this is the right place, Rachel, judging from the line up," said a tall, bearded man to one of his companions as they joined the line behind me.

"We are only halfway down the block," said Rachel with a warm smile. "Glad we came early."

"Canadians?" I asked, pointing to the Maple leaf on their packs. "I'm from Toronto."

"Ah, Toron'a," said the third person who introduced himself as Bill. "No, you're not."

I laughed. "The 't' always gives me away. I'm from Boston originally. A transplant."

"How'd you end up in Canada?" asked Rachel.

"Married a Canadian," I said.

"Is he here?" asked Rachel.

"Also divorced a Canadian," I said.

Turns out the three were old university friends and funny, in that way you only find in Canadians, but is hard to describe—charming sarcasm, perhaps. We chatted while waiting to register and I learned that they were leaving the following morning, a day before my planned departure. If I hadn't reserved a spot in Orisson part way up the mountain for September first, I might have changed my plans and walked with them to avoid walking alone. They'd be great company. I had never really traveled alone and I am embarrassed to admit, it made me anxious.

But I had decided to stay here two nights on purpose, to be able to land in the moment and when the hostel in town reopened, I met many people doing the same. Joseph, the innkeeper and host made a warm place to begin. One woman, Chrissy from Florida, (a woman who looked about half her stated age of sixty-four), had stayed four nights trying to screw up her courage to face the mountain.

Wanting to take off was just me panicking again. Pema Chödrön, a Buddhist teacher and one of my guides, has a good meditative exercise for these moments when you really want to just split. You simply stop and watch your breath, in and out, repeating Stay, gently to yourself until the storm, whatever it is, passes. Fast, effective and portable—I use it often and I used it then.

After just one day in Saint-Jean-Pied-de-Port, self-doubt was replaced by a feeling of genuine ease and freedom and I was so glad I had trusted my instinct at each choice point so far. I was even feeling a little sorry for the women with the suitcases. Even if I didn't have to worry about carrying the stuff because it was being transported to magically arrive at my door, if I had a suitcase nearby, I knew I'd be thinking about the stuff in it, because let's face it, I like stuff. *Will my stuff arrive or be lost? Will I wear the blue shirt or the green shirt or the white shirt?* Having almost nothing with me, I had almost nothing to worry about and was therefore free to experience the moment. Each morning, I knew I would wear the clean shirt and was free to spend the gained time doing anything else, including doing nothing at all, once I figured out how.

Now that is true freedom.

I spent two days wandering around the picturesque old town with new friends, Janet and Meg, two American women, learning how it was to have nothing to do, vacillating between feeling excited to get going one minute and nervous to go the next. We strolled past the colorful shops that lined the main street—fabric bolts in the windows of red, green, orange and yellow stripes, stalls full of handwoven espadrilles, their rope heels all piled one on top of the other, the pretty clay pots—and we left everything right where we found it, our packs carefully measured as they were. When we got to the corner store, full of huge woven sacks of spices, grains, nuts, dried fruit, we wandered in, beckoned by this feast for the senses. Variations of reds, browns and oranges lined the shelves, in a mix of textures and scents; it was intoxicating and a real pity we did not have a kitchen. We bought a pilgrim-size portion of nuts and dried fruit for three days and moved on.

Walking along the river, appreciating the red clay tile decorating the rooftops on the other bank, I said to Meg and Janet, "You know, as much as I love the cobblestone streets and all the little shops, my favorite thing about this place is the energy. It is buzzing. Can you feel it?"

"It's the pilgrims. The excitement is electric," said Janet.

"And the nerves are, too," said Meg. "But nerves in a good way."

"I feel like I want to get on with it, now, you know?" I said.

"One more sleep. One more beautiful dinner with Joseph. But, yeah, I want to get going, too," said Janet. "We are so lucky that the weather cleared. It sounded like the mountain was socked in with fog a few days ago."

The bells began ringing the hour and that reminded me I was still short some gear.

"Oh hey, I'd better go get those trekking poles before the shop closes," I said as I remembered an important errand. "I'll see you back for dinner."

Our lazy afternoon, my second in the town, was a good way to recover from what had transpired at the previous dinner, what would be one of many Camino coincidences yet to come.

. . .

That first night I arrived, after leaving the Canadians outside the pilgrim office, I found myself in the hostel, Beilari, sitting across the long wooden table from a woman about my age, Laura, who seemed distant and nervous, looking left to right, shying away from eye contact. She had saved a spot for someone and was clearly delighted when that person showed up, a radiant young woman, only a few years older than my own daughter. Laura greeted her with a kiss on the cheek, obvious affection between them and introduced her to me.

"This is my daughter, Kate," she said, beaming.

"Oh wow," I said. "You are walking with your mum?"

Didn't see that coming.

I imagined what my face must look like and tried to get the smile on my mouth to reach my eyes, but I am sure it was unsuccessful. (Fun fact, that is one way to tell if someone is lying—top of the face does not match bottom of the face.)

Laura answered for her daughter.

"When my husband died suddenly last year," Laura paused, trying to stop the tears that were coming. She continued after a moment, "I decided to do this pilgrimage to take his ashes. When I told Kate, she was worried about me."

A look of love passed between them, so many words unspoken and tears in their eyes.

"Well, of course I was, Mom," said Kate, squeezing her mom's hand. "You don't need to do this alone."

"She insisted on coming with me to Burgos," said Laura, "and then her sister will join me from Sarria," she paused, tearful. "I am so lucky to have them," she said.

You have no idea.

The room started to spin.

I wanted to get up and run and I hated myself for it. This poor woman just lost a man whom she described as the love of her life, but watching this unfold in front of me, the obvious love between her and her daughter, was like a steel blade in my heart. The woman was clearly gutted by her loss. And yet, I couldn't help thinking: *You have no idea how lucky you are.* We passed the noodles, the grilled eggplants, the wine and bread, and I listened to their beautiful story while my insides liquified. This was not the place for my story and so it remained, as ever, untold, turning to a cancer in the dark.

Devouring me.

Sitting in front of me was the picture of all I had lost. That sweetness between a mother and daughter, a sweetness we had for sixteen years; years we read books and talked and laughed at the kitchen table over tea and hot chocolate, afternoons after school when she would tell me all the latest, summers on Cape Cod, friends coming over and filling our happy, welcoming kitchen. Our home—mine and my daughter's—full of love. Watching every field hockey game, astonished at the possibility of injury. Going to every Improv competition she was in—she was so funny.

Was.

I talk about my daughter in the past tense because I don't know who she is anymore. Often, I don't even know where she is. On the bad days, I think maybe I imagined her. Imagined us. For four years, there had been a steady disappearance during the fallout of a high-conflict divorce, complicated by the addition of new relationships. Trying to stop her from vanishing was like trying to pin down a ghost.

I always assumed love would continue and one day I would sit with my adult daughter just like this, heart to heart. Like I did with my own mother, my sister with her daughters— it is what I knew. I couldn't even imagine it now. It was a fantasy.

. . .

I have a repeated nightmare that goes something like this: Beatrice and I are on a journey and it involves a ferry crossing. We park the car underneath where the vehicles are stored for the rough journey and go up to the deck.

Bea says to me, "Mum, I'm just going to go over there to hang out with my friends."

"Ok," I say, wrap my arms around her and kiss her on the forehead. "Be safe."

I spend the journey watching the new land come into view and the old recede. When it comes time to go back to the cars, I go all over the ferry looking for my daughter, calling her name, "Beatrice! Bea?"

I think perhaps she is already in the car, so I check there. All the other people are in their cars ready to disembark. In a panic, I run back up to the deck, now convinced she has gone overboard.

"Bea!?"

I grab a sailor by the arm and plead with him, "I've lost my daughter! I think she has gone overboard!"

Hysterical, as any mother who lost a child would be, but it was the only thing that made any sense.

He asks me to describe her and when I do, he says in an off-hand way, "Oh, her. Yeah, she got back off the ferry before we left port."

I stand there stunned, crushed: *My daughter is gone. How did this happen?*

I hear the man as if at a great distance though he stands next to me, "Listen, lady, you gotta move your car. People want to get off the ship."

Standing, immobilized. How do I go on? Where should I go? Forward? Backward? How do I go anywhere when my daughter is lost? Nothing made any sense.

In the endless nightmares, my heart found a hundred ways to lose my child. I have lost her in a crowd, in a dark forest, at a circus, and in one of those misnamed Fun Houses they have at amusement parks, where you never know what you are really seeing. I've lost her in a house that seemed like a real house, seemed like my house, but kept morphing into something unfamiliar, with doors and walls always shifting. Once she was kidnapped and driven away in a black truck driven by what looked like two huge junkyard dogs. I've had dreams in which she is behind a locked door and I am holding a key, but the key is broken. In one she was behind a thick wall of glass, carrying on with her life in a room full of strangers and I kept screaming and banging the glass to get her attention. She turned to look at me but didn't see me, a look of confusion on her face, like she knew she lost something but couldn't figure out what it was. Someone on the other side of the glass looked at me and said to Beatrice, "What is *she* doing here?" Beatrice shrugged and turned away from the glass. I woke up from that one with a scream stuck in my throat and soaked with sweat.

The ferry was the most devastating, however, because in this dream, she wasn't lost or coerced as she had been in the others. In this dream, she left of her own volition.

Even worse than having these dreams was waking from them to find that it was happening and there seemed to be nothing I could do to prevent it. Love was not enough to stop this horror.

. . .

Luckily, Laura and her sweet daughter departed the next morning, so I had a day to recover my emotional stability wandering around with Meg and Janet, putting myself back together like Humpty Dumpty. I chose my table mates carefully for the following dinner.

Unfortunately, Bridget departed with Laura and Kate. Bridget, an Irish woman a few years older than myself, had the energy of a Celtic seer—both deeply rooted in nature and connected to ethereal, unseen realms. I felt connected to her in only a matter of minutes in the Beilari garden on the first day and I missed her sparkling company the second night. After another beautiful meal, we all turned in early to prepare for the next morning. Perhaps, the excitement of the journey ahead woke me up and landed me in the kitchen with Rosemary, a Beilari volunteer, on the morning of my departure on the 1st of September. I didn't regret the missed sleep.

Kitchen Noises, Blog excerpt, September 1st
It is five in the morning and I have been awake since three-thirty, tossing and turning with worry about all manner of minutiae and finally decide to quietly slip out of my sleep sack and creep downstairs with my notebook. The old house is dark and creaky, the ancient wooden boards complaining under

my bare feet as I pick my way down from the third floor. All is shadow and quiet except for some soft snoring. I slip into the kitchen carefully, through the swinging French doors, groping in the dark for a light switch and manage to find one with a dimmer – just enough illumination to see. The long wooden table, laid with colorful linen and baskets waiting for bread, was set last night for the breakfast we will share this morning. The tick-tock of the old clock and the soft hum of the refrigerator keep me company.

I spot a little antique desk and banquette of sorts, so I curl up there, take out my notebook and let the thoughts come, trying to capture the beginning of my journey. Joseph comes to mind first, the hospitalero with his beautiful way of welcoming everyone and creating a safe container for sharing tender things. The chef, Mathieu, is like sunshine itself, with his brilliant, youthful delight and enthusiasm for everything and the fantastic vegetarian creations he produces each day, nourishing all. I think of Rosemary, who has come to volunteer for three weeks before she walks her own Camino, what a kind and generous spirit she has. I love the name Rosemary, the herb of remembrance, also used for purification and consecration. A good herb and a lovely person. As I start to write about her, she materializes, sweeping into the kitchen through the swinging doors.

Rosemary smiles when she sees me at the desk, maybe pleasantly surprised to have company at this hour while she sets up breakfast, something she has done here for the last two weeks. Or maybe she is smiling because there is often someone found here in the wee hours. I offer to help, but she declines saying she has a system and tells me to keep writing, handing me some fresh orange juice and a shawl of soft white wool to keep off the morning chill. I try to note as many of the kitchen details as I can because it is such a warm, homey place and I want to gather it all into my heart so I can return later to visit—the French kitchen doors, painted blue with shiny white egg door knobs, the colorful tiles, the old wooden bench worn down by many a pilgrim bottom, the white plaster walls and the rustic chandelier over the counter. The soft light, the simple white dishes, bowls of fresh fruit. And most of all, sweet Rosemary, who is trying not to talk so I can write, but can't help herself and, honestly, I would prefer to talk with her anyway. She is like a mischievous, benevolent pixie—luminous and full of fun. She reminds me of my dear friend Julie.

There is a rustling noise outside and a bag of freshly baked bread comes in the kitchen window. She turns, beaming at me, holding the bag to her nose, taking in the aroma.

"Every day," she says. "Fresh baked bread through this window. How amazing is that?"

Rosemary chats on and off as she gets the coffee pots perking, pouring the milk into bottles for the table, her head of dark curls now and then disappearing beneath the counter then poking back up again with a fresh thought, eyes sparkling. We are talking in whispers, even though the clanking of the utensils and bowls fills the little kitchen. The atmosphere in the kitchen reminds me of something Julie said to me when she was in her final days at home, dying after five years of battling with the cancer that stole her from the family who surrounded her. Her bedroom was just around the corner from the kitchen and she said how comforting it was that even while she was alone in her room, too ill to get up, she could hear the clanking of spoons and whistling of kettles, her bustling family just down the hall.

The comfort of kitchen noises making their way through the walls and down the hall, the sounds of home. Her family was together and though she could not continue with them, she said this helped her understand that they would be OK. Home. Making dinner, baking, tidying up, sharing food, laughter and conversation.

We can't hold onto anything, or anyone, but maybe if we really land in a moment in time, a moment that is infused with love, maybe we don't need to. Maybe it becomes part of us, a beautiful thread woven through us, making time irrelevant.

. . .

In the years before Beatrice started slipping away, she often came to Julie's with me—but back then she came everywhere with me—and though Julie's daughters were older, there was always warmth and an enthusiastic welcome for her. Every time Bea joined me there was a special baked treat for her— her favorite, vegan peanut butter cookies. That recipe in Julie's handwriting is plastered on the fridge at home and seeing it when I pass conjures her for me even years after they have both gone.

There is something mystical about someone's handwriting remaining after they have gone. I could sit on the floor for hours surrounded by my daughter's old schoolwork and other artefacts dug out of a dusty box—remnants salvaged from her childhood. It brought mornings back to life—the smell of pancakes, wiping the sticky syrup off her hands, popping a little note in her lunchbox, kissing the top of her sweet head and sending her off with a "Love you sweetpea. Have a great day!"

It broke my heart repeatedly, but I did it anyway, because it reminded me that I didn't imagine her.

Like a moth to the flame.

I realized Rosemary was talking and I dragged myself back out of the mist of reminiscing I had fallen into, brought on by the warmth and music of the kitchen. It seemed that she was mostly talking about breakfast prep, so I hadn't missed anything crucial.

I was curious about what inspired Rosemary to come here as a volunteer, because it is demanding work and she has said that she is thoroughly wrung out at the end of each day. She had some personal reasons for coming back to the Camino, it was not her first, but she said the impetus for starting this way, as a volunteer, was to begin with generosity. She was so full of gratitude for all she had already received that she wanted to start by giving back. It seemed like a beautiful gesture, but I wouldn't have a deep understanding of this spirit of the bountiful generosity of love until much, much later in my journey.

When Joseph breezed through the French doors and the energy changed, picking up speed, I took my leave. During the dinners, he reminded people—a room full of strangers—how to be with each other as a family, for many a lost practice, reminding us to look into the eyes when we raise our glass to toast, when we introduce ourselves to each other, to attempt to remember names. We served each other from communal bowls, just like a Sunday dinner, enquired if people had enough, set and cleared the table. We were not here on holiday to be catered to, but to learn and practice how to be.

Over those first two days, I realized how apart I was from any sense of family, uncomfortable even sharing a room with three people. I had become lost, isolated, in my unspoken grief. I had lost family for complicated and not so complicated reasons, but the reasons no longer mattered.

Later, I would come to understand how important it was to start this way. Although I was grateful for the hospitality, I did not fully appreciate how the experience in Saint-Jean-Pied-de-Port set the tone for the entire Camino until much later in my journey and how pivotal that experience was—magical even. It was a tiny, but mighty training ground, led by our guide, Joseph, a welcoming and a jumping off point, but it took me the whole journey to understand its significance.

. . .

At eight o'clock that last morning in Saint-Jean-Pied-de-Port, on September 1st, Rosemary and I were at the Sunday morning Pilgrims' Mass, a Basque singing Mass and we both stepped out a few minutes before it ended as it was sweltering inside the church. The Mass was a feast for the spirit, women on one side, men on the other, filling the church and our hearts with such gorgeous harmonies and passion, it all felt very much like a blessing, yet I was dripping with sweat before I even began my walk so decided it was time to go. I loitered around the outside of the church, which sits right beside the portal to the Way, nervous about leaving alone and feeling ridiculous for feeling nervous.

Where are the other pilgrims?

There was something about Rosemary standing out there with me, smiling, wishing me "Buen Camino," not rushing me or questioning why I was spinning my wheels. I felt like a small bird leaving a nest, like I was being patiently ushered out even as I resisted. I think it took ten minutes for me to get from the church door, through the portal and over the bridge, a journey that normally takes all of one minute. I was waiting for all these pilgrims I was promised to start pouring through the gate, but it was just me, looking back and Rosemary standing alone on the other side of the gate, smiling and waving, not forcing anything but patiently bearing witness to my departure. Eventually I had to just turn and walk before the moss started growing under my feet.

Over the next forty days, I would (seemingly) randomly bump into people I had met in the beginning, but once I went through the gates in Saint-Jean-Pied-de-Port, the one person I hoped I'd see before my journey ended never reappeared. Rosemary. My gentle guide at the threshold. She was planning to begin her walk less than one week after mine and I hoped our paths would cross so I could thank her properly, once I understood the significance, for adding such sweetness and wisdom as I stepped into the unknown. Never saw her again.

Continuing along the path, I was shocked that there was no one else walking with me. I wandered slowly, dawdled even, through the last of the village outskirts and up into the countryside, hoping to be overtaken by pilgrims, because the last thing I wanted was to be alone. Absolutely no one.

I didn't want to walk *with* anyone, I just wanted to see someone going in the same direction. Where were the hordes of people you read about and see in movies?

Not a one. I began to worry in earnest.

Am I late? Am I early? Am I actually on the wrong road?

In any event, I was alone.

Hauling myself along the eight-kilometer ascent, drenched with sweat, feeling the full weight of my pack, my heart pounding, I found myself full of questions. *If I am having this much trouble on the first day, what happens when one day lands on top of the next, thirty-nine more times? And where are all the pilgrims I was promised I would be swamped with? How is it that, on September 1st, supposedly one of the busiest days to begin the Camino in Saint-Jean-Pied-de-Port, I am hauling ass alone, up this goddamn mountain without a soul to witness as I keel over and die?*

I stopped under a tree and took off my backpack. Beads of sweat trickled down my spine and between my breasts. I retrieved an apple from my pack and took a long drink of water in between gasps for air. I looked around, scanning the countryside below.

Breathe.

It really was beautiful when I stopped panicking and started breathing. OK, so I was still panicking a little, but breathing had improved.

Everything will be fine.

I saw two people coming up behind me, way down the winding path, so apparently not the last living soul to have left Saint-Jean-Pied-de-Port. Nor am I on the wrong road.

What a relief.

As I ate my apple and gazed out over the rolling green farmland, I had to ask, why have I done this to myself? Honestly, what in the name of all that is holy possessed me to walk alone clear across Spain, carrying all my belongings on my out of shape, sweaty back?

Oh yes, now I remember.

I wanted to die.

Which is funny, because apparently, I didn't want to die today—an improvement already.

The Lotus, the Mud and the Mortal Wound
Why all this walking?

'No Mud, No Lotus' was one of Thich Nhat Hanh's many teachings. The worms, the darkness and decomposed plant life—in all that goopy gunk is the nourishment needed to thrive. Alas, we only want the beautiful blossom and are continuously trying to get rid of our own mud, the enriching debris that helps us grow.

We cannot have the flower without the fertilizer.

Pema Chödrön, Buddhist teacher and author of *Start Where You Are,* offers that the best way to enlightenment (big goals) is to look around you and all the muck you are standing in and that is where you will find your riches. Wherever you are, right now, is exactly the right spot to start waking up. You don't need to clean yourself up, fix your hair, or read five self-improvement books to be ready to begin.

Begin right here in your questionable sweatpants, bleary eyed or full of rage—whatever mess you've got going on—it is perfect.

The more you try to brush off the shit and the pain and all the horror that no one wants, the longer this whole thing is going to take, and the harder it will be. The seduction of escapism is not a mystery. And yet, it is not effective outside of the immediate and transient relief it provides, as sweet as that relief is.

So, back to the mud—my mud, specifically.

Not so long ago, way down in the jungles of Peru and deeply immersed in an Ayahuasca* ceremony, a formless messenger came through the pitch dark to whisper in my ear, "'Tis a mortal wound. You cannot survive it."

Well, that was dark.

Not that dark is unusual in shamanic ceremonies.

Of course, knowing the definition of both words—mortal and wound—I didn't really need more information, but I looked it up anyway, as one might if they were scanning for a more palatable result.

According to Wikipedia (because Webster's found it unnecessary to catalog), a mortal wound is an injury that will ultimately lead to a person's death. Not a revelation, I grant

---

* Ayahuasca is a traditional South American plant medicine containing the psychoactive compound DMT. It is used in indigenous spiritual ceremonies for healing, insight, and transformation. It is part of a broader system of health, ritual and guidance from experienced shamans or facilitators, deeply rooted in the cultural and spiritual traditions of the Amazon.

you, but I needed to see it. A festering wound. Doesn't seem like much at first, then the sepsis sets in and it is curtains, my friend.

It occurred to me that this message was not good news, but it didn't surprise me to receive it either. If you are harboring a mortal wound, you probably already know it. It also occurred to me that the certainty of death was more related to the lack of proper care than to the initial injury itself. This may or may not be true, I cannot say. I'm sure there are wounds that are simply not survivable and, though I thought I may in fact have one of these, it seemed like something one should at least attempt to overcome, especially if a messenger, even an unseen one, took the time to raise the alarm.

"Psst, friend, that thing you got, it is starting to rot," is important news and whether it came from the sweet, singing Shaman or the angel Azrael, it would be silly and almost disrespectful not to get up and do something.

At least try, for goodness' sake.

But the fact remains, it takes a lot of effort to do something when you are feeling hopeless, so, you really do have to want to save yourself. Unfortunately, for some time I was not sure I did, in fact, want to save myself. Wasn't sure there was any point.

There are many ways to lose your daughter. The way I lost my daughter was like a death, but not death, so hope always remained, even when it was just the faintest whisper. Hope and sorrow and rage, all at the same time, drained me of life, day after bewildered day, month after month and year after year, until I found myself teetering on the doorstep of self-harm as the only exit from the pain.

Her circumstances reminded me of the story of Briar Rose from a book her paternal grandmother gave her on her 1st birthday. It turned out to be like a prophecy. It was my daughter's favorite book, though I did not like to read it. We read stories all the time when she was little, often with her lying tucked under my arm in her bed, helping me to turn the pages.

She had no shortage of books to choose from, but when she would ask for that one, I would say, "Sweetpea, don't you want to read *Paperbag Princess* instead?" In that story, the girl realizes the prince is not terribly reliable and she deals with the dragon on her own, saving the prince as well as herself. Her clothes and hair are a mess, as she has more important things to concern herself with, like taming dragons. She knew she was strong and capable and she sure wasn't waiting around for someone to save her. That was the kind of message I wanted my daughter to have at such an impressionable age. Believe in yourself and don't be giving away your power.

One day, to my great amazement, Bea said to me, "Mummy, I know you don't like me to read stories about girls lying around asleep, waiting for some stupid prince to save them, but I just like the pretty pictures." She was probably five at the time. At least the message was getting through.

Her favorite part of the story was a beautiful rose hedge that popped up over the sleeping princess. This was originally a tale by the Brothers Grimm, of a beautiful girl who was cursed by the insulted thirteenth fairy and went to sleep on her fifteenth birthday, not to wake for one hundred years. There was nothing to be done about it. Many tried to wake her and were devoured by the hedge. The prince who finally bestowed the famous kiss just happened to arrive at the very time the curse was lifted. (Timing is everything, but of course he took the credit.)

My daughter made it to sixteen and, though not entirely asleep, she appears asleep—or at least unreachable—unable to recognize me as the same loving mother she had the whole rest of her childhood. This insidious change coincided with the aftermath of divorce. Of course, it was not her fault—it is never the child's fault. She was only a child trying to cope with an impossible situation in which she had no power.

That is what being alienated is like—your child (or the person you have lost) is alive, but she is inside a briar hedge that is impossible to breach. She can neither hear you nor see you, no matter what you do, until the curse is lifted, should you both survive long enough. Suspended.

A mother is not a prince and so is inclined to keep throwing herself into the thorns because her child is inside, hoping one day it will be the right day. All the while, the sleeping princess remains in the tower, engulfed by the hedge, inaccessible until the curse is lifted. But our life is not a fairy tale and we do not have one hundred years.

I had been fighting for her for years. Broke my heart again and again. I just didn't want to do it anymore. I couldn't go back into the briar hedge, nor could I walk away. That is the never-ending dilemma and the never-ending trauma.

The mortal wound.

Over the past several years, my ability to find meaning and experience joy had dwindled to just about zero. That is not my nature, nor is my nature constant sorrow. When joy does occur now, it is usually brought on by music or nature, arriving completely unexpected, drenching me, but is extraordinarily fleeting. A lightning bolt in the dark, an ephemeral reminder of something lost, but not quite the same as the real thing. With the interminable periods of nothingness in between, life becomes intolerable.

Suffocating in mud, year after year after year.

It could be said I was doing exactly what the teachers advised about starting where I found myself, not turning away from the pain and accepting the mud as, well, fertilizer. But five years of fertilizer? I'm not so sure that was the intention.

Turns out the protracted grief and trauma had me so immersed in the mud, had me so paralyzed, that I had let the other parts of me atrophy. All I could see was mud, no blue sky and that is not really the spirit of the teachings. At least not as I understood them.

Walking the Camino de Santiago was not a decision, but an unmistakable call. One day, I felt a magnetic pull to turn away from everything and everyone, put on a pack and walk back into the world. To disappear into the world and, by doing so, land in it. To just walk and walk and not stop walking until it was time to stop. I remember the exact moment so clearly that I can see myself, standing outside the house in Toronto, a bleak February day in 2018, stopped in my tracks by a powerful, visceral feeling of wanting to just go. It was a clear call to return home—not a physical home, but to a place of belonging. That was about as much as I understood at the time. It took some effort to restrain myself until I was more prepared physically and psychologically. Luckily, during that time of preparation, I remembered the Camino.

A decade before that moment on the sidewalk, I was visiting my friend, Julie, at one of her little garden parties. Her friend Michael was there (who as it turned out was a philosopher, a musician and a pilgrim) and he was regaling us with stories of a pilgrimage he took to Santiago de Compostela. He probably talked about the history, as that would be his way, of the bones of the apostle and of the long history, but I didn't register much of that. He had a recording with him of Oliver Schroer, a Canadian musician who had recently died and he played it for us as we sat mesmerized by the music and the fire. Simply called *Camino,* it was the collection of recordings he had made with his violin all along the way, as he walked from Saint-Jean-Pied-de-Port to Santiago de Compostela.

It was the most beautiful music I had ever heard. It landed in my heart that evening and it stayed there all those years like a flickering lamp. The music was all yearning and longing and yet also full of joy and gratitude.

And so it was that an important seed was planted in Julie's Garden that evening and, just when I needed it, ten years later, that seed began sending up tiny shoots. I was indeed starting exactly where I found myself, still in the mud to be sure, but now looking up, toward the light.

The blessing of that experience on the sidewalk, a year before I left, was understanding that beneath the trauma, beneath the fog of prolonged grief and the blinding fire of rage, existed a calm, reliable presence who could be trusted to find the way home. To find the way back to the land of the living. Somehow, in that first moment when I heard the call, I knew the way would be through the simplicity of walking.

By the time the Camino resurfaced in my mind, I was not sure that 800 kilometers would be nearly far enough.

Stepping toward Grace

"Come, come whoever you are, wanderer, worshiper,
lover of leaving, it doesn't matter. Ours is not a caravan
of despair. Come, even if you have broken your vows
a hundred times. Come, come again, come."
Rumi

The walk on that first day to Orisson was difficult, but the reward was spectacular. I was pleased to not have had a heart attack on the short but steep climb and it was a great lesson in listening to my body.

Stop and breathe. Eat an apple. Look around.

The bonus later that day at the top of the climb, was a sprawling, sunny patio, overlooking the mountains where I reunited with new friends from Beilari—Meg, Janet and Liza—and met lots of new people, all gathering over cold beer on a hot day. This would become an important part of the journey, not so much the beer (abundant though it was), but these watering holes to connect and reconnect with other pilgrims. I was remembering how to talk to people, how to be with people, skills that had withered in the last few years, the disconnection a symptom of managing life with trauma.

Orisson has a famous ritual during a communal dinner in the dining hall, where people stand up one by one and say who they are, where they are from and why they've come. Once again, I listen to other stories of grief and hope, but this is not the place for mine, not in this cavernous place with all these strangers. I passed on the invitation to share and, before long, it was time to hit the hay and prepare for the rest of the long hike through the mountains the following day.

One of my bunkmates from the UK hadn't realized there would be shared rooms.

"What are you lot doin' in my room?" said a tall, bearded man in his fifties named Elliot.

He appeared to be unpleasantly surprised and scowled as he looked around the room at the other three of us. He turned to his traveling companion for an explanation, "May—did you know about this?"

I thought he was joking—English humour.

He wasn't.

That explained the jeans.

Apparently, his aunt May had planned the whole pilgrimage and he was late to join, only planning on a week of walking. It made for quite an entertaining first evening on the road.

"Oh, I see," I said. "So May, you had planned this for a year?"

"Two," she said, grinning, as she tossed her sleep sack on the top bunk. "I've dreamt of it for years."

"Two, right. And you decided to join her, when?" I asked, looking at Elliot, who was still coming to grips with where he had landed, opening and closing the locker.

"Last week" she said. "While I was packing my kit on the table."

"So, this is how it's going to go then," he said casting his gaze around the room. "We walk for hours, get sunburned and end up at a dormitory full of strangers to sleep in what can only be described as... rustic conditions. Brilliant."

Seemed he needed a bit more time to land.

"He's still processing," said May.

Before the lights went out, Elliot peered out from his bunk, addressing us all at once and said, "Don't tell me any of you lot snore?"

We all cracked up laughing, including Elliot, who had mostly stopped scowling, his wicked sense of humour gradually emerging.

The next morning, we were all up and dressed and out of our rooms early, so early the sun hadn't yet risen. I met May out by the water fountain.

"Where's Elliot?" I asked.

"He insisted on a shower," said May.

The showers, coin-operated in Orisson, were always done in the afternoon, after walking.

"It seems your Elliot goes his own way," I said.

"Oh, that he does. Are you heading out now?" asked May.

"I think so. I've been just waiting for it to be light enough," I said.

"If you wait for us, you may be awhile. And I am moving pretty slow. But you're welcome," she said. "If we don't see you, we'll catch up at the next stop."

We exchanged WhatsApp contact information and May went in to collect Elliot. I filled my water bottle from the fountain, a soft pink began to infuse the clouds resting softly on the distant mountains. I hung back to appreciate the moment, feeling blessed, excited and a tiny bit nervous, which seemed to be the new normal for me.

It was tempting to linger, to hang back so I could walk with my new friends, but something pushed me forward and I am so glad it did. I would have been pleasantly distracted by my buoyant companions, Elliot and May, chatting and laughing, but in doing so, I would have missed a precious gift waiting for me.

Depending on when one sets out, there is often a clump of people coming out of the *refugio* at Orisson, but after a kilometer, I found myself with relative solitude. I could usually see someone in the distance, but it felt solitary up in the mountains. Before too long, maybe a few kilometers, there is a statue of the Blessed Mother, set back at a bend in the road as you climb into the mountains. Not grand and imposing, she is just a simple shrine sitting alone against a backdrop of rolling mountains. The day I visited, the distant mountains were shrouded in fog, which created an otherworldly feeling.

As I walked off the path into the pasture, I noted a change in energy. I didn't come to this shrine with any agenda—in fact I had only ever heard about it in passing—so I was surprised to find myself weeping. Bursting with gratitude for all those I loved, especially for the women in my life and grateful also for whatever spirits had helped me climb out of my darkness and get at least this far. I sat at the foot of the shrine with my notebook and poured out prayers for my dear, fragile old mother, for my beloved faraway daughter, for my oldest sister who has been like a mother to me and for my sisters' spirits.

I eventually re-joined the path, in full appreciation of how fortunate I was to be on this journey. I was so full of thanksgiving, the steps themselves became a prayer. I walked forward reminding myself gently and often not to hurry. *Be still and go slowly.*

What happened to me next up there in the Pyrenees, winding through the mountains? I don't know that I'll ever be sure.

Just after visiting the shrine and pouring my heart out, I rounded a corner and found myself alone in the mountains and I stopped, collecting my surroundings way up in those sprawling green hills.

With sheep on my right side, horses on my left, there was nothing and no one else around me, just the path ahead and behind as far as the eye could see. I felt the solid ground under my feet and a spell of silence but for the wind whistling and the cow bells tinkling.

An enchantment.

Normally, this would unnerve me, this utter aloneness out in the wide world, but I felt none of that old fear. As I stood there, for the first time noticing everything around me, I felt scooped up by some unseen presence and a feeling of divine connection filled me entirely and that is when I received the message for the first time.

It was as if the presence I felt was speaking to me: *You have never been alone. There is no such thing.*

Awed, I continued into the mountains.

I rounded another corner, with just the tick, tick of my walking sticks, the wind and distant cow bells as my companions and I was greeted with an enormous beauty—

green hills rolling in all directions, blue morning sky, horses happily grazing. Birds soaring.

It was magnificent.

Then, an invitation from above, below and all around me: *Here you go darling, all this beauty is yours and it has always been here, waiting for you. You only need to walk into it. Come. Come!*

Can it be this easy?

Well, it was just ridiculous, the whole thing. Has this beauty been here all along? Have I been standing in it, blind and numb? And was there actually a Spirit visiting me, because this defied explanation. How have I gone from nearly slayed by grief, to crying with joy and gratitude on the second day? The second day. How?

Nothing is impossible.

I laughed out loud, swinging my arms wide, shouting, "Thanks for waiting for me!"

Hello Joy.

For quite some time, I was laughing and crying simultaneously, snot running from my nose. A mess. Yes, good to have walked alone.

Day Two on my mission to Restore Joy and I find myself awestruck and filled with joy and thanksgiving. Repentance too, for being so blind with grief I could not see the abundance gifted to me every day. I could only see what I had lost.

For hours, I was visited by a benevolent presence—the Universe, God—call it what suits you, I don't believe what we call it matters. It was the most profoundly moving experience I have ever had. It was as if I had walked through some unseen doorway into the staggering beauty of what has always been right here before me.

With every step that day, I let go of my attachment to anything that interfered with this spirit of Joy. With every step, it felt as if I had walked a bit further out of my grave and into my life and a bit further into myself, back into my own skin. I felt a gentle reconnection between my spirit and my flesh, a little like what the Shamans call a soul retrieval.* My spirit had just been returned home to my body. And it felt as if I was having a Welcome Home party and the guests were the sheep, the cows, the horses, the birds soaring overhead, the wind and the other hikers in the distance.

I am not alone and I never have been alone.

The feeling of aloneness was simply an illusion.

Up and up, into the mountains I walked, off the road into the fog, into the wind, past the fountain of Roland, into Spain and eventually down and down the steep path through the

---

* When trauma becomes unbearable, some traditions believe the Spirit or soul, flies from the body and the Shaman's job is to go out to the spirit world and find it and reconnect it to its physical body.

old birch forest, which delivered me finally to the monastery at Roncesvalles, the first rebirth, dying to my old life and reborn as a pilgrim, a seeker, with weeks of wonder spread out before me. My mission to restore the capacity for Joy, which I assumed would take all forty days, granted, as if I had made a wish on a magic lamp.

What more could there possibly be? It can't be that easy, can it?

With the Camino, you may not get what you expect, or even what you want, but if you follow the signs, the arrows and the whispers, you will get exactly what you need. Perhaps I needed my spirit back in my body to make a spiritual journey. Just a guess, but it made sense to me.

What I do know is that I had a sudden and complete awareness of my own delusion that I am separate. I had taken the first steps toward my intention—to Restore Joy—and, for simplicity let's call it the Universe, offered an abundance of blessings at the doorway in recognition. Faith, trust and courage, rewarded immediately, without asking, just for showing up. A gift, given out of love. I didn't have to walk a hundred miles. I didn't need to fall to my knees. I just needed to screw up enough courage to find my way to the portal, cross the threshold and allow myself to be met. It was astonishing.

It felt like Grace.

Guardian of the Bells

"Compassion is a verb. It is an action.
It is not just something you feel. You must transform
your compassion into a force that can heal the world."
Thich Nhat Hanh

Stopping overnight in Orisson had left me fresh to take my time and because I had time, I had no impulse to rush through the mountains and was open to receiving. A few hours after my humbling visitation from the Divine, I stopped for a picnic at the shepherd hut, the tiny building which is a refuge for pilgrims who find themselves up in the mountains when the weather turns. The feeling of joy and gratitude (and also wonder) was still with me, but the wind had picked up, so I didn't linger past my snack of bread, cheese and nuts procured in St. Jean.

Scampering along the path, not far from the hut, there is a choice; go left or go right. I was thinking back to the instructions at the pilgrim office and was pretty sure they mentioned that this choice was an important one, as one way is a tricky scramble. I tried to make out the signage, but it was unclear, so I waited a few minutes to see what other folks did and all I could determine was that most of the pilgrims looked equally unsure and went equally in both directions. I suppose I could have asked someone, but instead, I flipped a coin and headed off to the left. (Good thing I am not writing a guidebook.)

It was an attention getting steep descent (thank you hiking poles) through the forest to Roncesvalles. Turns out the advice was to go right.

I love the woods. I really do. And this birch and pine forest was beautiful. Even so, I don't love being alone in the woods. I especially don't like being alone in the woods when I feel like I am being watched. Every now and then I would stop and listen. No footsteps near me. No pilgrims now that the one trio of Germans had sailed straight past me, and yet, I had the strangest feeling of not being alone. I don't mean that expansive, connected feeling of not being alone I had earlier in the day. This was more like wandering into a scary movie.

Like wandering right into the haunted woods.

Haunted enough that I doubled my speed. (Outrunning the phantom menace probably explained why my knees were in such bad shape the next day.)

When the haunted woods deposited me into Roncesvalles, I looked around for Elliot and May from Orisson but there was no sign of them. Check-in was organized and I made my way to the third floor and down the long hall to find my four-bed bunk compartment, which is where I met Kay, unrolling her sleep sack.

The monastery houses hundreds and the church offers a Pilgrim Mass for all. I didn't have an intention to go to a Mass, but my new bunkmate Kay from California was looking for company and it was a good reason to stop drinking wine on the patio with the other six revelers I had connected with, so I joined her. That is when I learned that her husband had died earlier that year and she was carrying his ashes.

She spoke of a deep ambivalence she held about the church. My relationship with the church was neither ambivalent nor complicated. I was raised Catholic and hadn't practiced for many years simply because it didn't make sense for me. My mother would say that I lost my faith. I would say, I didn't believe anymore. It was a point of contention we usually avoided.

I generally preferred to visit the churches when there was no Mass, but the Pilgrim Blessings could be quite nice. Kay was there for her husband, to accept the blessing for his spirit and I was only there for Kay, so I sent my blessing her way, as I had had my blessing in the mountains.

The following morning, we set off on the long walk to Zubiri together, though Kay was faster than me and I urged her not to wait for me, especially as, predictably, my knee was acting up from yesterday's self-imposed nonsense. When I noticed people starting to jog past me in the early afternoon, I thought I should enquire.

"I've noticed people suddenly starting to hurry," I said to a harried looking pilgrim as she buzzed toward me. "Do you know why?" I asked, thinking maybe a weather change, though the sky looked blue.

"No beds in Zubiri," she answered, panting. "Municipal is closed."

"Ok thanks," I said to her back as she was already several steps ahead.

At first, I wasn't too worried, but when I thought back to my reservation, I was pretty sure it said that you had to call the day before or your reservation could be given away after three pm. I didn't have a phone plan yet, so I didn't call. I checked the time and discovered it was 2:30. That is when I started to hustle.

And a frantic scramble it was, further injuring myself running down loose shale for kilometers (what I later learned is called the Dragon's back) carrying fifteen pounds to score what may have been one of the last beds in town. I made it to the stone bridge at the entrance to Zubiri at three o'clock, only to discover my reserved albergue was way over on the far side of town. I truly wanted to cry.

I dragged (and I mean dragged) myself through the streets, singularly focused and collapsed in the front yard, ready to beg to sleep on the dirt if my bed was gone, but it was not. I got a bunk and a hot meal and a hot shower and I was so grateful. My wants were simplifying.

Given all that drama and to rest my aching body, I decided on a short walk the following day from Zubiri to Zabaldika, to the Sisters of the Sacred Heart, as I had heard it was a special place for quiet reflection and I certainly needed some.

I was surprised to meet my friends from Orisson, Elliot and May, at a coffee stop along the morning's walk out of Zubiri (and what a particular joy it is to spy companions at a rest stop when you thought you had lost them).

"Did you reserve a place in Pamplona?" May asked.

"A friend back home told me there is a wonderful church just off the path ahead and you can stay there if there is space. That's today's plan," I said.

"That is not a plan, love," said Elliot. "In fact I'd say that sounds like a bit of a disaster."

"So, I take it you don't want to join me," I said. "There is a bell you can ring."

"Oh good. A bell. Do you know they have hotels in Pamplona? Like proper hotels," he said. "Have you got something against comfort?"

"Well, the church sounds perfect. I just hope they have a bed," I said.

"Have you reserved nothing?" he asked. I shook my head in reply.

"Oh. My. God. May, she is worse than you," he said.

"I'd love to see it," said May.

"Fine," said Elliot. "I'd love to see a church that is nicer than a hotel. Absolutely fascinating."

We walked along the river, catching up on the last days adventures. Elliot seemed to have landed and was enjoying the journey after the shock of Orisson passed. It was about six kilometers on when May spied the sign that pointed the way off the road to Zabaldika.

"You're joking," said Elliot. "It's a goat path."

Up the dusty, rocky slope from the road, the small convent and church appeared, blending seamlessly into the landscape. There seemed to be no one there, so Elliot and I went straight upstairs to ring the bell, leaving May, who wanted a break from climbing, on a bench in the empty courtyard.

I love church bells. Love, love, love them and cannot resist.

Up the narrow, stone, spiral staircase we went, seeing not a soul and landing in an old wooden loft with two bells, one of them broken. The other had a sign next to it that read: *Please, ring bell once or twice ONLY and pause for reflection,* in several languages.

Unfortunate that this needed to be stated so explicitly, but I could imagine people racing up there, mindlessly banging away on the bells with the poor nuns suffering below. Having a deep reverence for bells, the musical call of we mortals to the divine, I cannot fathom abusing them this way.

After a beautiful moment of ringing reflection, we descended the stairs and were confronted by the guardian of the bells, a woman who later turned out to be a nun. Well, she was always a nun, but not dressed in typical nun fashion (ignorant of me, yes), so I assumed she was a *hospitalera* (a volunteer host), which was my great mistake. Well, I should say, one of my many mistakes.

There was no hello.

"Did you visit the chapel?" she asked pointedly.

Never have I seen a gaze so piercing. Formidable. Like she could read not only my mind, but view the contents of my heart and, quite frankly, found them both lacking. Unnerving, to say the least.

"Uh, not yet," I stammered. "We were just up..."

"Up in the bells! Yes, yes, I know! You ring the bell before you visit the church? The sisters do not like this. They will be upset with you," she said sharply, while handing both of us a guide in English for the small chapel.

This was not an auspicious beginning for what I had hoped would be a restorative stay. It was more like time travel to the third grade.

Elliot and May left rather quickly, with a chuckle and a "Good luck," tossed over their shoulders. We promised to catch up down the road.

When the Sister realized that I intended to stay there that evening, our relationship only deteriorated. It was not the warmest welcome I've ever received.

A few more people gathered in the courtyard, including Hannah, a young German woman I had met briefly in the monastery in Roncesvalles, and a family from England who I kept bumping into that morning. They all hoped to stay that night.

The Sister was having none of it.

"It is early," she said. "You can keep going to Pamplona and there you will find a place."

Hannah and I explained we were staying for spiritual reasons and she seemed to be considering that, so the English family followed suit and said the same. Their thirty-year-old son persisted in talking to my breasts all afternoon while we waited to hear our fate, so I have my doubts about the veracity of his plea for spiritual sanctuary, but I was staying in my lane. I was there on purpose and was committed to doing whatever was necessary to convince the sister of my worthiness. Honestly, it felt like an audition for a bed.

At one point, the nun looked at me and asked sharply, "When the pilgrims come this evening looking for a bed, you will drive them to Pamplona?"

In my desperation to build some kind of bridge between us, I totally missed the nuance and responded with excitement, "Of course!"

I thought it was marvellous they had a car and I wondered if I was insured to drive over here, but I would be happy to give them a lift to Pamplona. What a great idea. She walked away shaking her head, clearly exhausted by my stupidity. After an hour or two, we were accepted, even the pervy, boob-staring man-boy dressed in camo and suddenly the refuge was full before three pm.

When the first person who arrived after we were at capacity heard there was no bed for her and she would need to push on to Pamplona with her enormous backpack, I came to understand why the Sister was shooing the early arrivals away. Given that just yesterday I had stumbled into a town worried my bed was given away and near tears thinking I could not possibly walk another step, I understood the pilgrim's crestfallen expression and I felt awful. Nevertheless, my recently revived spirit needed to be here, I couldn't say why, but I was sure of it, so I did not give up my bed. But the lesson sure landed hard and I vowed to never take more than I needed, of anything, freshly and viscerally aware as I was that when you take something, it is no longer available for someone else. Very humbling. I immediately went to the kitchen and did as much as I could to help Augustine, the hospitalero from Argentina, prepare dinner for everyone. A joy and a penance.

After the communal dinner, reflections and prayers were offered in the church with the Sister, heretofore in disguise (well, disguised to me at least). Sharing was encouraged and, unlike Orisson, it felt like a safe place to share tender things, but my heart was so full the tears were choking me. I was afraid if I spoke, I would sob incoherently and as I felt I had created enough scenes for one day, I just wept quietly amongst strangers, reading together the Beatitudes of the Pilgrims. I wasn't even sure what I might say that would express the depth of my gratitude, the sense of sacred presence that I felt. I was just too raw.

I left the Sister a thank you note the next morning, so she knew the bed wasn't wasted on me. I told her that I had been full of grief and came to the Camino because I had wanted very much to die and each of these experiences, like the breath of spirit in the mountains, was bringing me back to life a bit at a time, stitching me back together and my gratitude for that was beyond words.

I also told her that I eventually understood about her guarding the place, about her fierce compassion. I pictured her in my mind as an unswayable gargoyle in human form, but I was afraid she would take that the wrong way, so I kept my imaginings to myself on that point. Never miss an opportunity to keep your mouth shut.

Hannah and I made the short walk together in the morning to Pamplona and didn't see another soul for the first hour, so we had lots of time to chat. Pilgrims get to serious topics quickly here. She told me about losing her father when she was quite young, how enraged she was at the loss and how much she admired her mother for how she supported her. Under rage is usually grief, so her mum held her safe while she screamed and let her pound her fists into a pillow, never insisting she feel anything other than exactly what she felt. Hannah told me of her intention to use her experience of early loss as a volunteer to support other children who have lost parents and she is all of twenty-four herself, just a few years older than my own daughter.

She asked me about Beatrice, so I told her about our struggles. I told her how excruciating it was to not really be part of her life for the last several years, to have become a ghost mama. Gutting. And how worried I was that my daughter had become torn in two navigating the fallout of divorce, but she wouldn't talk to me about it and it was not safe for me to talk to her father, so I had stopped trying.

Like Hannah, Bea has her own grief and rage, but I knew more about Hannah's than I did my own daughter's and that fueled both my sadness and my feeling of impotence. My new walking companion was so open about her own pain and something about her being so close to my daughter's age, I don't know, it all came pouring out, my bewilderment, frustration, sorrow and yes, anger.

What interesting walking companions—she a daughter who has lost a parent and me a parent who has lost a daughter. This is how the Camino works. People appear, people you might never interact with in your everyday life and it feels as if they have been sent to you, like benevolent messengers. No wonder people talk about Camino angels.

We got to the municipal albergue of Jesus y Maria in Pamplona by noon and got two bunks. I thought it would be interesting to sleep in a church, never considering that it meant sharing the sleeping space with a hundred people snoring, drooling and farting—all enjoying the acoustics for which churches are known. Met some fascinating people, but I did not stay two nights, as you might imagine.

I had anticipated wanting to stay two nights in Pamplona, especially as it was the haunt of Ernest Hemingway and tragically, I am a romantic, but the homage to bullfighting everywhere was making me feel unwell and the noise of the city felt out of place with my mood. It is a beautiful place and, in another context, I would have liked to stay longer, but I was up and out before dawn. Hannah miraculously remained sound asleep in the din, the contents of the albergue drifting out past her bunk as she slumbered and I left her to enjoy her rest as we had agreed the night before, being undecided as she was on whether to leave town.

I AM ALIVE!

Update from a picnic table in Puente la Reina

Blog Excerpt. September 6th

It has been just over a week since I flew from Toronto and I had meant to be in touch days ago, alas, I have been a little busy here sorting out the basics. I mean really basic. Essentials such as: Is my knee blown out? Where can I find vegetarian food that is not thrice boiled from a frozen bag or a slice of cheese on dry bread? Should I be concerned about these spots on my arm? Where can I wash my clothes? Is it OK that I now smell my clothes to decide if they are clean? What happens when there are no beds at the end of a long day? How can I convince this nun to let me stay here? How can I settle my nerves when every day is the Great Camino Bed Race? Toilets, water, etc. Packing and unpacking and walking day after day. I have used everything I have stuffed into this backpack and wish only for—I guess nothing now that I consider it.

I am glad that I ignored good advice and packed what I was told was a redundant long-sleeve black merino shirt, as I am now using the blue one as a towel. Best guess is my microfiber towel blew away today on a blustery, mostly solo, twenty-five kilometre walk to Puente La Reina. It was early this morning when I left Pamplona and I had it pinned to my pack to dry in the sun—a common practice. I'm sure I saw it when I stopped at the steel sculpture on Alto de Perdon (the Hill of Forgiveness). The inscription at the sculpture that sits atop the hill, 756 meters above sea level, the biggest climb since the Pyrenees, is *"Donde se cruza el camino del viento con el de las estrellas"*: Where the path of the wind crosses that of the stars. Makes sense that things would blow away in a place they call the path of the wind. Forty wind turbines lined the way up, I was buffeted for kilometers and at the top stood in absolutely bracing blasts and yet I did not think, at any point on this walk, to tuck things away. (Shocking that I have only lost a towel so far.) Nevertheless, this incredibly beautiful day—the blue skies, the sunshine and waving fields—all well worth the towel.

I have no idea what is happening tomorrow. I am inclined to stay in this charming town another day, but I am also inclined to push on. We will see. That is what Hannah says, "We will see." Who knows, why plan?

So many new friends. So many beautiful people. Here is something that surprises me—part of the feeling of rush I am wrestling with is related to everyone having different paces and timelines and priorities which means you lose people who have become friends. The desire to hang onto people and the willingness to abort my own priorities to do so, is lurking just under the surface, but I resist. Sometimes people reappear down the road and sometimes they don't. Once I accept the flow, I see that every day brings a new beginning, a new journey with new challenges and new faces. I meet wonderful people every day. It is a lesson in allowing everything to pass, at least for the moment.

Such a magical place, full of gifts and lessons and I have been walking for less than one week. I am shocked at how little we need to live happily and at how we are constantly trying to acquire the wrong things. Already I dream of returning home and unburdening myself of unnecessary belongings.

I hope someone has told my mother that I am frequently in a church at least twice a day now. She would like that. Time to vacate this picnic table so I can buy a new towel before the shops close. The replacement towel dried in less than two hours and is a shirt once again. Who knows what it will become tomorrow...we will see.

And all that fuss about my foot over the summer was for nothing. Well, it is a little swollen, but considering how painful my knee is, I barely notice the foot. Just waiting on the blisters now.

PREPARATION, ALL SORTS

Journal notes before setting off, August 2019

Travel light, they say. It is a long walk and the heavier your pack, the more strain on your knees and feet. No more than ten percent of your body weight goes on your back, or you are asking for trouble.

Funny. I had never much thought about my feet. Do you think about your feet? Every now and then, I look down and think, *Maybe I should paint those toenails,* but I don't and immediately forget them. Poor feet, doing all that work and not getting an ounce of thanks.

Suddenly I am thinking about them all the time. In fact, I would say an hour doesn't go by that I have not, at least once, thought about my feet. Specifically, about my right foot. Obsessively.

People post and compare their packing lists in online forums. I am talking about conversations with complete strangers that include the best types of socks and underwear (which is quite pivotal in many ways). Getting caught up in these details takes my mind off the astonishingly inconvenient fact that my right foot is still not working. Haven't done a long practice walk in over seven weeks and I miss my new weekly walking group companions.

In the last month, I have taken my foot to the doctor, had it X-rayed, visited the chiropodist to have it cast for an orthotic, suffered adjusting to the orthotic, thrown most of my beloved shoes out (and later the orthotic), bought uncomfortable hiking sandals that were "good" for me and subsequently abandoned those. I have gone to the physiotherapist to have my gait re-checked and my cuboid freed. No change in the pain. The acupuncturist hooked me up (literally) and adjusted my fire and water.

"Too much fire."

Don't I know it, Doc, don't I know it. I gamely ingested an herbal medicine I really did not understand. My energy may have rebalanced, but it most certainly did not change my foot.

I went back to the walk-in (ironic) clinic and insisted on antibiotics just in case I had, oh, I don't know, a little bit of flesh-eating bacteria. I was refused (and it must be said, reasonably so). We engaged in what was probably a frustrating conversation on both sides about what infection typically looks like. Red, hot, shiny, etc. Of course, I knew this.

But you see, my dog scratched me a month ago and, well, you never know.

I was given another series of x-rays instead. No fracture.

When I visited the massage therapist, he put a lot of pressure on that foot and it felt great. So, it seems I am already fairly certain my foot is not broken. Before leaving the clinic, I make an appointment with the podiatrist, in case he has the answer. Later that week he tells me that my orthotic is inappropriate as it is turning my right foot toward the painful joint and that I likely have arthritis. He thought my joint was hot. Which immediately brought me back to asking for antibiotics for my, now proven, bacterial infection. He gave me a prescription for anti-inflammatories instead and suggested I see a rheumatologist. I'm sure he is wrong, so I don't bother, but I hang onto the prescription, just in case. I line up an appointment at the Cleveland Clinic for a sports medicine specialist, get a referral to an osteopath and hobble away.

Honestly, I am surprised none of these people referred me to psychiatry.

At some point, as I am regurgitating the small horror of my foot, I mention to someone that the massage was the only thing that seemed to bring any relief. *Hey, why the heck haven't I made another appointment with the massage therapist?* Which I did. As he was pushing on the front of my right leg, away from the pain, I felt a deep pressure, traveling all the way down to my foot.

"Wow, I sure feel that," I said. "Is that connected to something?"

What a question. Of course, it is connected to something. Everything is connected.

He is a wise man of nearly seventy years and he doesn't laugh at me. He is also a shiatsu practitioner.

"The stomach," he said. "Does that mean something to you?"

I meant connected to my foot, but OK, I'll bite.

"Well, it has been a bit off in the last month," I said. "I feel like I am getting ulcers."

You see where this is going, right?

Suddenly, I am talking about the thing I don't want to think about or talk about and it is not my foot. I'll talk about my damn foot all day long. What I am talking about now is the thing it seems I can do nothing to change. The thing it seems I must try to bear without imploding and turning to ash: the mortal wound. He listens to me with kindness and because he is wise, offers no easy solutions. He knows there aren't any.

For a solid month, all I could talk about has been my foot. I am boring even myself with all this nonsense. I try not to talk about it, but if someone brings it up—OK, even remotely—I go on an unstoppable recount of the whole ridiculous saga. It strikes me that trauma is like that, or some phases of it. It can make you a bit narcissistic, just temporarily. All you can think about is this mind-boggling, soul-crushing pain you are in and, if you don't pay for a whole lot of therapy (and sometimes even if you do), it can become a bad habit to pour it all over everyone else.

"Did I tell you about my (insert extraordinarily painful thing here)?"

"Yes, yes you did. (insert polite exhaustion) Several times."

Unlike other situations in which talking helps, reliving trauma does not help relieve the distress but makes it grow. Talking can be like fanning a flame. But just like the relentless foot saga I tormented all of Toronto with, sometimes you just can't stop yourself. You become so incapacitated with thinking about yourself, drowning in your own personal horrors, that you are entirely unable to see that these people before you might have a little pain, too. Or, possibly, a little joy. And it does not occur to you, even remotely, that they too, may want to share it.

I do recall, and this is a bit embarrassing to admit, that a few months prior, I did pointedly ask the Universe for physical pain on my Camino. Asked for it. People talked about blisters and injuries and making best efforts to avoid them and I said, out loud mind you, "Good. I want pain."

I mean, truly, you have to shake your head at that level of myopic stupidity. The Camino is a long bloody walk to begin with a painful anything. Nevertheless, I wanted physical pain to take my mind off the relentless, unbearable emotional pain, because the latter was true suffering. And when you sincerely ask the Universe to intervene, it has been my experience that it does. So, I have no one to blame but myself.

Be careful what you ask for, my friends.

La Rioja Threshold

"It is a joy to be hidden, but a disaster not to be found."
DW Winnicott

Despite all the poor preparation and calls to the gods for difficulties and challenges, I was at least prepared (or determined, or lucky) enough to get (almost) to La Rioja, beautiful land of rolling vineyards.

From that sunny picnic table in Puenta la Reina on September 6th, I taxied to Estella for an unexpected invitation to a farewell dinner for Elliot, who was returning home the next day. Food, friends, music and wine, *al fresco*. It was well worth the slight headache the following day.

There was a fall chill in the air, but the moon was lighting up the plaza and the Rioja wine was warming our blood. The conversation was sprawling, the food was indulgent and the plaza was full of happy people, pilgrims as well as locals.

Elliot's friends, Richard and Amanda, were also leaving the following day, though they were off on another wild adventure and entertained us all with the plans they had for a safari. Elliot was returning to work in England, reluctantly. We had such fun together the few times we saw each other, I was sad to see him go. There was something about this unexpected friendship that felt like a step toward bringing me back to life.

"Now remember, Colleen, comfort is not a crime," he said laughing at me good-naturedly. "And be careful to read the signs before you ring any bells. Can't have you enraging the clergy."

We all laughed as Elliot regaled the others with the story of our misstep in Zabaldika and my offer to "drive the pilgrims" to Pamplona. It was way, way past pilgrim bedtime when we finally turned in.

May had invited me to stay in her swanky, rented apartment that night, so I had everything with me, which tempted me, ever so slightly, to just walk on from Estella and pretend a taxi ride was the same as a walk. I didn't feel good about it in the end and returned to yesterday's true end, Puenta la Reina, by bus so I wouldn't miss anything. Having everything with me did give me the opportunity to clean absolutely everything in her washer/dryer and that was blissful enough.

Lo and behold, at the bus stop, didn't I find sweet Vincent, his brother Chris and their eighty-year-old father—the French family I had met in Saint-Jean-Pied-de-Port. I hadn't seen them since the mad dash into Zubiri. It was wild the way people disappear and reappear when you least expect it. What a treat that was and I would have missed it had I (a) declined the invitation to dinner—which I had considered based on too much perceived effort and a latent (very latent) desire to be sensible or (b) decided to cheat today and walk on to the next town. All these serendipitous encounters reminded me of that old movie, *Sliding Doors* from 1998, and it had me thinking of all the possible Camino trajectories with all these people walking in the same direction on the same path, making multiple small and not so small changes to their plans every day. It was mind-boggling and left me feeling a little greedy to want to live all of them.

Hampered somewhat by my sluggish condition, I was surprised how much I enjoyed the sunny walk to the medieval hilltop village of Cirauqui. It was probably only eight kilometers from Puenta la Reina and I arrived ridiculously early, but it was such a pleasure to sit on the terrace, writing and chatting with new people—a delightful way to pass an afternoon. Decorated with colorful floor tiles, interesting sculptures and paintings all over, there clearly was an artist in residence. Apart from periodic church bells, the tiny village was nearly silent and there was precious little to do, which was perfect. We shared dinner by candlelight in a wine cellar, chattering in all manner of mixed languages, but with enough shared understanding to connect. It was a good day and I slept like a rock.

Because I had had a short day getting there, I left early the next morning, early enough that the headlamp I left home to save weight (so I could pack critical pilgrim essentials such as sugar scrub and lipstick) would have been useful. Luckily, I bumped into another pilgrim trying to pick his way out of the tangled streets.

My new Kiwi friend, Big Jim, got us turned in the right direction and off we went. He was a tall man, maybe six and a half feet, linebacker shoulders and had a booming voice. He told me that his first day was fifty kilometers. Given that information, along with the length of his legs, I had to assume he was slowing down for me, but he was nice company.

I passed Estella for the second time—it was a little strange to have already been there—and not far from there was the famous wine fountain of Irache. The funny thing is, not many people want wine at eleven in the morning, especially in the middle of a very long walk, nevertheless, Jim filled his entire water bottle. This did not turn out well for him later.

Just past the fountain is the studio of an ironworker who created the most extraordinary pieces, mostly Camino related. His work was gorgeous, but I couldn't even accommodate a tiny bit of jewelry with the way my feet were starting to feel. I needed to get rid of stuff, not collect it, no matter how beautiful. So, I left the earrings and the pendant and everything else I coveted, and we moved on.

Both Jim and I end up staying at Villamayor de Monjardin, a place neither of us intended to stay. My plans, what little I had, seemed to be out the window. A collection of expectant pilgrims was developing on the albergue stone patio and down the steps into the road, so we joined them.

At first, I noticed some bristling as the pilgrims who came before us wanted to be absolutely certain we understood the lineup of packs was meant to indicate arrival order. By the time we got there, it was getting close to full and you could see people as they arrived silently counting the packs in front of theirs "...18, 19, 20..." to be sure they would have a bed. After the count, we relaxed and many of us contributed to an impromptu picnic while we loitered in the blistering sun. It was a long old wait, but well worth it. While we waited, we enjoyed shared apples, boiled eggs, cheese and bread pulled from our backpacks and Big Jim went to get some cans of beer. These are nice moments when we are held fast together by the simple fact that there is simply nowhere else to go and nothing to do and often leads to entertaining stories from the road.

I looked up from a conversation I was having with Jim and a young woman from the Netherlands, Emma, and I was surprised to see Hannah coming up the road.

"Hannah!" I said, both of us smiling broadly.

"I thought you were so far ahead of me. I'm so happy to see you!" she said, running up and throwing her arms around me.

She went over to put her pack in the lineup, with all eyes on her to be sure she knew where the end of the line was. She got the last bed if the count was right.

Jim introduced himself and passed her a cold beer and we got caught up on her last few days. She had slept so soundly in Pamplona that the volunteers had to rouse her at nine so they could clean. It turned out we were just a half step apart the whole way. We likely caught up with each other because I needed an easy half day after the festivities in Estella with Elliot and May.

This hostel, run by a Dutch community, was extraordinary. The volunteers tended to pilgrims in a way that I can only describe as people giving themselves over to God's work. It reminded me of stories of Jesus (cool, hippie Jesus)—humble and generous. They had us sit down while they poured us saltwater foot baths, indulged us with fresh lemon water to drink, popped blisters and managed other injuries, like it was their absolute pleasure to do so. Like there was nowhere they would prefer to be but holding and tending to our sweaty feet. It was nothing short of genuine, authentic, beautiful compassion.

While volunteers Dan and Mary tended to feet, the volunteers in the kitchen prepared a fantastic meal for more than fifty pilgrims—lentil stew with fresh herbs, crusty bread and a fresh salad with none of those weird white asparagus. When even the hostel's overflow spaces were full, the man who runs the place took the final eight people back to his own home. As promised, no one was sent away without something to eat and drink and someplace to sleep.

They offered a communal meditation after dinner in a cozy little room that was more like a cave, lit by candles. What with all the tending, the exhaustion and the water bottle from Irache full of wine, Big Jim fell soundly asleep on my shoulder during the meditation, snoring away. It was a bit awkward, not going to lie, but after all I had received, it seemed the least I could do to let him rest right where he was, so I did.

These volunteers, my goodness. It was not just what they did, but the way they did all these things. Full of love. And I never would have experienced it if I hadn't been late, trotting off with a hangover from Puente la Reina—the dark is in the light and the light is in the dark. Best to be open to the full banquet and the accompanying mess of the human condition. Walking into all these lessons, I was a humble and grateful student.

I couldn't say what it meant to the other pilgrims to be met in this way by the hospitaleros in the Dutch hostel, but for me it was a pivotal moment in restoring me to myself, like what happened in the mountains and later in Zabaldika, only this time, by fellow humans, of being seen and being found, being received and tended by total strangers and they have my eternal gratitude.

I felt found.

. . .

To be traumatized is to exist alone in a time warp. Though the world outside is moving and turning and making trips around the sun, the traumatized person is frozen in time, excommunicated from their fellow humans. Although the term excommunicated typically refers to religious exile, the word means simply to be outside of communion with others. Banish, shun, ostracize—whatever you call it, and however it has come about, it is a devastatingly cruel punishment. Unbearable.

DW Winnicott, a pediatrician and psychoanalyst said, "It is a joy to be hidden, but a disaster not to be found."

It is said trauma that happens in relationship needs to heal in relationship. Not necessarily in the relationship that caused it, which is often impossible, but in relationship with another; for that, one needs to allow themselves to be seen again. That is a difficult thing to do after so much practice of hiding, especially when hiding has served the function of survival. Based on my short time on the Camino Francés, I'd say it is difficult not to be found here. It is such a strange and deeply beautiful experience, to be seen and tended to, to begin to feel real again.

. . .

From Villamayor de Monjardin, many of us left for Torres del Rio. It seemed a new traveling family was beginning to form. We were the people who gravitated toward the in-between, small, off-guidebook places as beds were less scarce and there was a titch less frenzy. Passing briefly through Los Arcos, I stopped in the plaza by the church long enough to refuel with a *bocadillo* (ubiquitous dry sandwich) and write down a few words before they all slid away from me.

People I had met in the beginning of the journey had largely dispersed. People I believed to be behind me were already ahead by days and people who I was sure were ahead, were days behind. It is difficult to let go.

Kay, my spirited bunkmate from California who walked with me from Roncesvalles to Zubiri, possibly the fittest of all, a fitness trainer who gave us tips on stretching and use of poles, was lying in the hospital in Estella, getting stabilized to fly home with a herniated disc in her lower back—she couldn't even stand. May, who speaks a bit of Spanish, was there when it happened and she had to call the ambulance as well as update Kay's daughter from the hospital. May said she was devastated not to be able to complete the journey, having planned to take her husband's ashes to the Iron Cross.

Surely the woman who broke her ankle on day two is long gone home, but the woman who broke her finger probably continued. People struggled with blisters, colds, muscle and tendon strains. Some people leapfrogged ahead with transport assistance because they hoped to get in front of the bed race, or due to injury, or lagged behind for the same reasons. You just can't hold onto people. We help as best we can, but we must continue to walk our own way.

Walking, walking and more walking.

The day we walked from Torres del Rio into Logroño, it seemed a purple sky was chasing us most of the way and, though it didn't really rain, it was unnerving. When it was getting particularly scary, I stopped into a cafe, thinking

I might wait out the storm over a *café con leche*, along with the two local fellas enjoying some vino at nine in the morning.

Eventually you must push on and hope for the best. I had heard that there was a *parroquial albergue* in Logroño, a *donativo* with a communal meal and, remembering how precious Zabaldika was, I really hoped to spend an evening there. Hannah decided to join me.

"Do you want to sign up for the communal dinner?" I asked Hannah as I checked in at the old rectory office. There were only twenty spaces but over thirty beds so some folks would make their way to tapas alley for dinner.

"Yes, of course," she said.

After showers and laundry, we found ourselves in the kitchen, chopping tomatoes and tearing lettuce with a few French pilgrims. We had a simple meal together, sitting at a long table, breaking bread in the traditional way with our temporary pilgrim family. While we were cleaning up, the priest, José, chatted with us.

"You know, this practice, the old way of donativo, sharing, is something that is at risk. Too many people want hotels. Everything predictable. They don't understand what they miss," he said, passing dishes through the kitchen window.

"This is my favorite part of the Camino," I said.

And I meant it. The Camino wouldn't be the same healing journey without it.

"Yes," he said. "This is how we remember that we are not strangers. We are brothers and sisters. Family. It is the spirit of *communitas*. We don't need much, but we need each other."

"Better than the Parador," said one of the French women, referring to the five-star luxury hotel stay. She laughed as she swung her dishrag in the air with a flourish.

This *communitas* is what I had been feeling all along the way, especially back in the Dutch albergue. It is what Joseph had been gently teaching in Beilari at the very beginning. Now I had a word for it. I retreated to my bed feeling restored in body and spirit.

From there we walked separately through the beginnings of La Rioja, through the rolling fields and through the town of Navarrete, past the red hills and eventually meeting up in Ventosa, where we made a fantastic supper from a vending machine, created from a box of *tomate frisa*, a can of chickpeas, a small bag of fusilli, a couple packets of butter our new Belgian friend, Olivier, pulled from his pack with a bag of shredded cheese. Oh, and of course, the wine, which, believe it or not, was pretty good. Except for the butter and pack cheese, it was all from the vending machine.

Incredible.

Hannah (who was beginning to feel very much like a Camino daughter), and Olivier continued with me to Azofra. I have no idea why Hannah wanted to hang out with someone old enough to be her mother, but I sure loved her company.

Olivier and I became fast friends in that Dutch hostel when I gave him my bottom bunk. His feet hurt, which made climbing the metal rungs terribly painful and, miraculously, my feet were not so bad that night. I remembered the Sister at the convent in Zabaldika and the lesson of only taking what we need and I happily offered to switch spots. I believe Oliver and I are now friends for life, illustrating, amongst other things, the importance of a bottom bunk on the Camino.

Azofra, another sleepy town, resulted in limited dinner options once again, so we collected whatever was fresh in a little Mom and Pop shop down the street and went back to the *albergue* communal kitchen to put together something we called Camino ratatouille. The cheese—which isn't typically in ratatouille to the best of my knowledge—really pulled the whole thing together.

These quiet places away from the frenzy of the pilgrim rush give everything time and space to settle. To be still. There is nothing to do, nowhere to go. Perfect.

That pain I ridiculously asked the Universe for months earlier faithfully complied and then some. The initial foot pain wasn't even the issue anymore, though it remained (the pain and the foot), but it was nothing compared to whatever was going on with my heels. I was pretty sure several blisters were bubbling up under my toes, as well. I gave them a little extra love in the garden after our ratatouille feast, hoping the extra care would help them carry me to Grañon the next day.

"No extra kilometers on the scenic route for you my loves," I whispered to them as I massaged Voltaren and foot grease into them.

Grañon, a famous place by Camino standards, is a wonderful donation-based *albergue* attached to San Juan Bautista church from the 9th century and a most unusual experience. We arrived a little later than usual as I had to take some breaks for my heels, though weirdly each rest break seemed to make them worse. We showed up a bit desperate to know there was a bed, especially after walking up the stone stairway past a recessed window filled with more than three dozen pairs of pilgrim shoes. I stopped and looked at Hannah, eyeing all the shoes.

"I don't care if they put me in the yard," I said. "I don't have another step left in me."

Hannah got to the top of the stairs first, arriving on a landing with six other people, two of whom seemed to be in training. I realized we were coming up on mid-month, which is the time the *hospitaleros* (or volunteers) changeover, usually with an overlap day. I could see into the main room, which was all warm wood, with a fireplace in the corner and someone playing the guitar. A jug of lemon water stood on the table next to the volunteers with "Welcome Home. Help yourself." in five different languages.

Hannah turned and looked at me, smiling, "I like it here," she said quietly. "Now, if only there is a bed."

Not only was there a place to sleep, but there was also a job. As soon as the Canadian volunteer checked us in, she said, "I am sure you two want to get settled, but we really would like to take our two new volunteers out for lunch and we'll be a couple hours. Would you mind terribly giving us a hand?"

"No, of course not. We'd love to help," I said, with nods of agreement from Hannah.

And just like that, we became temporary *hospitaleras*. I couldn't believe the speed with which they ran out the door, tossing us the keys and some sparse instructions (years later, as a hospitalera myself, I would come to understand this reaction viscerally). Granted, we were given the easy part of the job, greeting people and showing them where to put their stuff, that sort of thing, but we enjoyed it immensely. What a joy it was to receive and welcome people. Though it was brief, it was a real taste of how people arrive; some easy, some a bit desperate, some with blisters, hunger, or thirst. Most delighted there is a bed (or in this case, a mat).

As it happened, we arrived on Friday the 13th and didn't all the lights go out as the priest was saying a Mass in this ancient church that we accessed by what looked to me like a secret passage from the bunk room. Several candles had to be lit so he could read, which made me wonder how it was that a priest of his accumulated years and, one must assume, practice, didn't have the words memorized. And there is not a bit of cheek in this, but it seemed that at this stage, he could just wing it, no? Maybe that is not done in a Catholic Mass.

More importantly, he was a lovely, gentle man. After dinner, he led a candlelit reflection in the choir loft where all were invited to share and he gave everyone a hug as we left. The space was held with such compassion, a sense of true safety was created, as I had seen in other circles and people spoke openly about what was in their hearts. I could only say, "I am here for my daughter," before the tears came up to choke me, but people nodded in understanding and just being in the presence of this energy was healing. The lights remained out until morning, so we (over fifty people) prepared, organized and ate dinner together by candlelight—salad, spaghetti, bread, wine—and had a candlelit dish brigade to wash up as well. Someone picked up the guitar and there was some singing. It was all so wonderful I didn't even mind the sleeping mat on the bare wood floor for one night.

However, I didn't realize the next night in Tosantos, another *donativo*, was also to be on mats. I minded that a little—old bones.

The family running the place in Tosantos was full of kindness. They made a homemade paella in a huge pan for the extended family of twenty pilgrims and held an evening reflection under the eaves in the loft of the little house for the twelve of us who stayed with them. The invitation was to write a prayer (or wish, or hope) for yourself or some personal intention, but what you take turns reading are the prayers from the pilgrims who came twenty-two days before you (the estimated days to arrive in Santiago from this point), creating a feeling of connection to "strangers" ahead and behind on the road.

Hannah read a prayer from a pilgrim named Rob. "I have come this far and still my anger is with me. It is such a heavy burden and I am starting to feel hopeless. May the rest of my walk help me release it. Not to forgive, but to let it go. I want to be free."

Olivier read one in French I didn't understand but the people who did smiled.

My turn. "I am grateful for this body that carries me every day, my resilient spirit, my clear mind. I have been given so much on this road, I can't ask for more, so my prayer is for those I walk with and for you who hear this—may you all be well, may you know peace and love. Ultreia, Amy."

By the time we got around the circle, the room was full of reverence. I folded a prayer for my daughter and deposited it in the box to be picked up by unknown hands and read to a room of strangers in three week's time.

"I walk with a grief that never really leaves me. My daughter is becoming a ghost. So am I. I don't know what else to do. I came here because I was ready to give up—I guess I could use some hope. Some strength. Maybe a miracle? And for my daughter to be well."

The whole experience was a balm for the spirit, but after two nights on thin floor mats, the top bunk in the crowded municipal *albergue* in Agés—covered only with a paper sheet and positioned directly over a noisy, snoring Englishman—felt like the height of luxury, like landing in one of those Paradors.

Being told I got the very last bed when my legs would go no further also contributed to my appreciation. I wasn't too worried about the snoring, but I did offer to put my backpack behind his back once he was asleep. Granted, the packs are not actually allowed on the bed because of bedbugs, but there are not any extra pillows, which would be ideal.

My new friend laughed nervously at my offer, in a non-committal, she's not serious way and slipped away to brush his teeth. I was deadly serious, but I am sure you'd agree that I could not in good conscience interpret this as consent, so I refrained.

There were worse situations in town. This is the town where there is an option to sleep in a hay loft, on the hay, which sounds rather romantic until you think about it. People the next day were complaining about the bug bites, which to be perfectly honest, I didn't think of, but of course if you are sleeping on hay in a barn, you might find some bugs in there with you. Perhaps the bugs don't appreciate it either, to be fair. One more reason to be glad of my humble top bunk.

Hannah and I had split up to walk separately after Grañon because my legs were hurting and I didn't want to slow her down, but in true Camino magic, my bunk in Agés, the last bed in town (aside from the hay), was the one next to hers. No need to plan. I sent a note to Elliot back in England to let him know about the wonderful things that can happen when you don't make a plan. He was not impressed.

The Way takes us to Burgos next. I have heard this walk into the city described as relentless, never-ending and brutal. It was a bit of a worry, but I walked with the knowledge that I was giving myself the indulgence of an Airbnb apartment for two nights and was pretty darn excited about that. I would drag myself there by any means and deal with the damage when I landed.

I had been drying myself with t-shirts for many days (never did get that towel), had no tips on my poles, was running out of toothpaste and lost all sense of my timeframe, but other than that, and considering what others have experienced, all remained well and manageable.

The Meseta

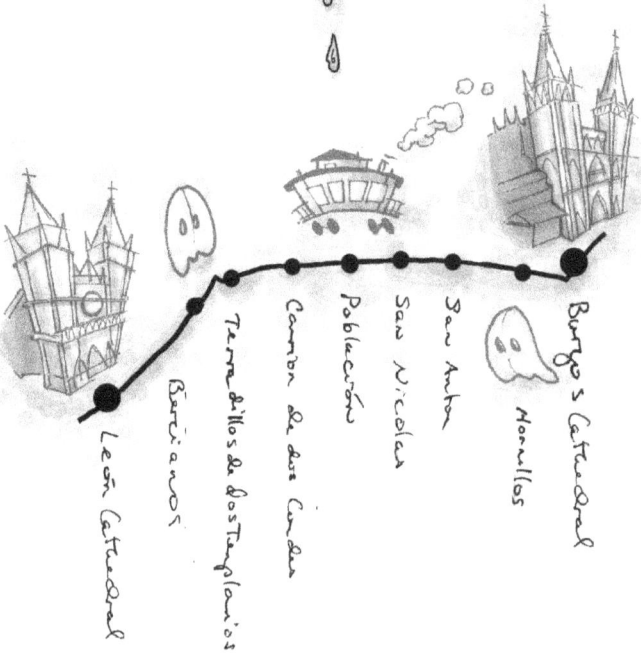

León Cathedral
Bercianos
Terradillos de los Templarios
Carrión de los Condes
Población
San Nicolás
San Antón
Hornillos
Burgos Cathedral

GETTING UNSTUCK
IN THE MIDDLE
WITH YOU

(the Meseta)

Sometimes Joy is a Bathtub

Burgos, threshold of the Meseta

Blog Excerpt. September 17th

It may take a small army to remove me from this perfect little apartment next to the cathedral. Oh, and it is perfect. Last night I looked out my window and thought I had landed in a Van Gogh painting. Stunning.

Barely made it here yesterday with a huge blister on my heel, three more on my toes and that strange heel impediment which has only deteriorated, likely Achilles related, (double tendonitis perhaps) that makes it look and feel like I am walking on tree trunks. Or like Frankenstein. I stumbled into town (yes, again) with Richard, an old friend from Orisson, who I happened to meet at the exact juncture where the path divides and you must choose between the industrial roadway, which is the main path, or the river option, which looked to be empty of pilgrims as far as I could see. With my feet this bad, there would likely be no help if I needed it on the river. I was fretting about whether I was feeling confident enough to break off onto the lesser traveled river route alone when I saw him at the end of the bridge, contemplating the same thing. That is just the kind of magical assistance that happens here. I am sure the softer ground along the river and the good conversation made the long walk into town more enjoyable. And it was a long old walk from Agés.

Maria, my rental host, let me in a bit early, bless her. Up five flights of stairs with my backpack and my dead feet I trudged, wondering if my appearance was going to impact my Airbnb guest rating. She showed me around the apartment, moving from the hall past the bedroom, through the little kitchen into the sitting room and started to show me how to work the TV. I smiled, "No necessita, señora. Gracias." I went straight to the bathroom to be sure I knew how to work the taps and I was delighted to see a plug—I have been told that sometimes the tubs have no plugs, for reasons that escape me. But believe me, I was prepared to use a sock and whatever else I could find.

She wasn't out the door five minutes before all my clothes were spinning in the washer and I was delighting in an exquisitely hot, private bath. I may have started peeling clothes off as she was backing out of the doorway. Band-Aids and Compeed plasters falling off all the blisters and my sore muscles drinking in whatever lavender smelling salt substance I had generously poured in the water. At one farmacia, they had said it was just for feet, the other had said it was OK for the whole body. Still not sure what I soaked in, but it seems to have been some kind of fancy Epsom salts. At least I think so. I could be treating my entire body for foot fungus, who knows, but it sure smells good, whatever it is.

Oh, that precious feeling when you know there isn't one other place in the world you would rather be. If I were standing in the kitchen, I would see the side of the massive white cathedral and all the people milling about underneath. From the bathroom, I can hear people outside the window roaming about the city, the sun having just reappeared after an afternoon rain shower and I am in my tub. One hundred and eighty-two Canadian dollars buys me the option to stay in this tub for two nights and two days. I consider bringing the bottle of wine Maria has kindly left me straight into the bathroom, but decide I also want to cook something, which requires getting out and putting on the one thing that didn't go in the wash, the black dress that also serves as pajamas.

As I prepared dinner, I reflected on an earlier invitation to join a group of six renting a larger apartment and I looked around my tiny kitchen and smiled. It seems I am beginning to become attuned to myself, at long last.

I cannot express how deeply content I am right here in this moment and it is not an exaggeration when I say that I believe I will need to be forcibly removed from lovely Burgos. I have been so engaged in self-restoration, I have not made enough time to explore the city and I still need to squeeze in a massage. And there are all those shops with tempting, beautiful autumn clothes in the window—tweed jackets, sweaters, shiny boots— distant echoes from another life.

I am on the threshold of the Meseta, getting ready to walk up into the sky and I want to be sure my body is healed. The Meseta, the iconic high plains, expansive and unsheltered, is part of the Camino many a pilgrim skip. I have been looking forward to it. Who doesn't want to walk in the sky?

Maybe I will stay another day. Just one. Maybe if I move from my decadent apartment to a hostel tomorrow night, it will ease me back onto the simplicity of the Pilgrim Road.

Yes, that is what I will do. Just one more night.

Two sleeps and three baths in this small slice of heaven has been a simple and exquisite joy. The sun is shining, my clothes are clean, I am certainly clean, my blister is shrinking and I am going to make another café con leche in my tiny, blissfully solitary kitchen

.

Treat yourself sweetly my friends. You all deserve it.

But first, a word about time.

A Word About Time

In *Zen Mind, Beginners Mind,* Shunryu Suzuki tells us: "You may say, 'I must do something this afternoon' but actually there is no 'this afternoon' ... At one o'clock you will eat your lunch. To eat your lunch is, itself, one o'clock."

Many scholars say that time is a product of the mind and our relationship to what we think of as time becomes corrupt. Teachers such as Thich Nhat Hanh and John O'Donohue speak about our perversion of time, that we allow time to become a bully. Pema Chödrön, advises there is no time to lose. I have often hoped that time is an illusion that we simply cannot understand.

In my grief, I have engaged in some unhealthy attachment to time. Exquisitely unhealthy, in fact. Calendar day counting and clock watching, adding, subtracting and treating time as a balance sheet. Losing the present by mourning over what has been lost and cannot ever be retrieved. Without time travel, we cannot change the past.

I wonder if everyone who loves stories of time travel has something or someone important they wish to retrieve? I cannot get enough time travel stories.

Oh, for those moments, to go back and make a different choice.

To have seen the danger.

Or perhaps everything is happening all at once? Is it true that a mother and child cannot be separated even by time and space as they share some of each other's cells? I know I can feel my own child in my arms if I really concentrate, I can see her smile, hear her voice. The possibility that there is no such thing as time is a comfort.

The Meseta is a place where time stands still. Under the expansive sky, you walk and walk and it seems you have gone nowhere at all. Is that what makes some uncomfortable about the Meseta?

There is a teaching that if one can stay in the present moment, going neither forward nor back, not rushing, nowhere to go, that what we experience as time expands. This is a real struggle, but I have done it (on occasion) and I know it to be true. When one is present, time does stand still—and you feel that you have gained time. In the Meseta, staying in the present is very much staying with your mind, minding your mind, but not *becoming* your mind.

. . .

Maybe just now, whatever 'now' is, you are becoming anxious with all this talk about time, thinking, "This is taking a lot of time. When is this going to end so we may return to the story?"

And so, we shall return, but because time is irrelevant, we will pop forward from Burgos to The Caboose.

Cacophony on the Camino Caboose

Somewhere in the middle

- still September -

four days into the Meseta

At whatever ungodly hour of the morning it was, I finally acquiesced to being awake after some interminable period of flipping and flopping, wrestled my legs from my narrow sleeping sack, rather dramatically flung them over the side of the bed and complained bitterly.

"Here we fucking go again."

The hostel, attached to a bustling restaurant, looked so nice when we checked in yesterday and it must be said that a midway pilgrim gets excited about the prospect of passing a pleasant evening, in a clean, welcoming space. This place had sleeping berths like train compartments instead of bunk beds—a Camino Caboose. It was like having your own tiny room, even if none of them were entirely enclosed. There were only ten of us, so how bad could it be?

Well...

Let me just say that over these last three weeks, this is the first time I have understood what people suffer when earplugs don't seem to work for them. I have never in my life, not even from my brother-in-law who used to shake the house with the racket he produced, have I ever heard snoring like this. Never. It can't be helped, I understand that.

Well, flipping people on their side and wedging a pillow behind their back sometimes helps, but strangers are understandably shocked by this kind of interference while they are asleep,* so not really an option, my earlier suggestion of wedging a pack behind a large Englishman in Agés several sleeps back notwithstanding. Even he, sleeping in the bunk underneath mine, who alerted me to the potential sound bath I was about to receive, even he was not this bad. Just a bit of white noise through the plugs. No sleep sacrificed.

The caboose, I don't know, perhaps it was some kind of crazy acoustics, but it was epic. Later, everyone blamed the Irish guy, poor Jack, with the CPAP machine and the hearing impairment, but I heard at least three distinct snores

---

* I know someone who did this on the first night in a dark bunk room. Not well received. Go figure.

throughout the night and, though it did turn into a bizarre sort of call and response, I can assure you, they were not harmonizing. I am certain Jack was one of them, but only one. Pretty sure the father and son, both named Roderic, were also involved—you'll meet them later. It was a mad cacophony. Maybe I had three hours of sleep total and I absolutely accept that in communal living this will happen from time to time, that it is part of the bargain.

However...

When the Lead Snorer gets up at 4:30 in the morning, belabors his toilette with wild abandon, returns to his berth and pulls what he must imagine to be a soundproof curtain closed to rustle through one thousand crinkly plastic bags in his pack looking for, one can only assume, a peanut, or his last ibuprofen, you'd have to say, this would test the spirit of Camino generosity.

My patience and sense of humor officially left the station. I should have gotten up to help him find whatever the hell he was looking for because Lord knows I was now wide-awake listening to the performance of his departure.

Where are you going at this hour, Jack? Even the sun is still sleeping for three more hours. Where is the fire?

After much cursing and muttering, I found myself standing at the caboose albergue door, fully dressed, backpack on and poles in hand, staring out into the dark, wondering whether to push off blindly or not. I was now in possession of a headlamp, thanks to Richard in Burgos who had a spare (I offered my unused sugar scrub as a trade, but he politely declined). Even with the light, I still preferred not wandering around before sunrise. While I was contemplating my choices, my new Meseta friend Frankie wandered down the hall wearing nothing but flip flops and his fluorescent orange underwear, his wild hair combed with a pork chop, apparently.

Looking like he just survived a crash and didn't know where he was, said "What the hell was that? Did you guys hear that?"

Yes. Yes, we did, Frankie. I think the very dead Saint James himself heard that.

As ridiculous as that was, the previous two evenings were utterly sublime, so my feeling was that a balance was struck.

But backing right up and returning to linear time that has been ignored almost entirely (perhaps the Camino is a curative for our attachment to time), we return to September 20th, four days before the Caboose, as I struggled to leave the shining white city of Burgos where I fell in love with a bathtub.

Early Meseta

Burgos for two nights turned out to be one night too little, as I suspected, so I took my English friend May up on a kind offer to share her apartment and her washer (once again) making it three nights in Burgos and a pack full of clean clothes to continue my onward journey. We celebrated the last night with dinner for a dozen pilgrims under the stars in the square, complete with tapas, paella and vino. Several of us, including Richard, had been there a few days, so I knew I wasn't the only one under the spell. It is a hard city to leave.

It wasn't just the beauty and the bathtub, but also the energy felt so bright—like a mini-Santiago—a meeting spot for old friends, for sharing of stories, laughter and rest. Many pilgrims begin or end their walk here as well. Hannah was one of those people, so it was time to say a final farewell to her as she had walked the remainder of the Way a year earlier. Her journey was complete in Burgos and mine had hundreds more kilometers ahead. There was something unexpected and healing about our time together. I loved feeling a bit like a mum again, walking beside her, sharing confidences. It reminded me what my relationship with my own daughter might have grown into if it hadn't been unnaturally interupted. A bittersweet moment.

"Well your mother will be glad to see you," I said.

"Yes, I talked to her this morning. She is planning a welcome home dinner for me," said Hannah, smiling.

"You are lucky to have each other," I said, with a lump in my throat.

"I know that, even more now," she said. "Your daughter is lucky to have you, too. You are a good mum. I think Bea will remember who you are. Maybe she needs some time."

"Maybe," I said, not at all sure of that but grateful for her kindness.

"I will miss you," we said at the same time with one final hug goodbye in the square.

As I watched her walk away toward the bus station, I wrestled with not lingering on the idea that Beatrice and I would have done this walk together in some parallel universe that didn't include the alienation after divorce. We had shared so much and experienced such joy in the past before it all came to a grinding halt.

The feeling of "unfair" is not a healthy place to wander into and that is where I was headed so I pulled myself out. Many of us have situations in our lives that feel unfair or unjust, when we feel something has been stolen from us and it is just not helpful to dwell there. Instead, I thought about my time with Hannah, that she wanted to walk with me for some reason, that she sought my counsel, that we enjoyed our time together.

It helped me remember that although I am not a perfect person, I am not by any stretch, a bad mother. That was just the gaslighting. The time together with Hannah reminded me that whatever has happened between me and my daughter is not because I am a bad person and that was important, because it lurks in the back of my mind, always looking for evidence to convict me. I am not sure what our time together did for Hannah, but for me, it was healing beyond measure.

I knew I was going to miss her, my Camino daughter.

After pulling myself away from the Burgos enchantment, I had a beautiful walk up to Hornillos, the beginning of the Meseta. Not much happening for me in Hornillos, but this is where I met Caboose Frankie of the orange underpants for the first time, who became a friend and a few other fun people I didn't see again, including Queenie from Ireland.

Queenie was grand, so she was, with her head of long red curls, her buoyant laugh, her bewitching Irish accent and her giant purple valise, which I must elaborate on later, as it certainly was an unusual sight. She was full of herself, in the best possible way, and full of life. It was a delightful evening.

The next two days were short walks as they were destination focused.

The first, San Anton, rustic old ruins, was a monastery donativo, to the south of the path. The dramatic remains of a stone archway crossed the road, but what was left habitable of the ancient building were the tiny rooms out the back in the courtyard. And there were beds (yay), but no electricity or hot water. The dormitory was a tiny room carved into the ruins, adjoining the kitchen, the only other room. We were just seven pilgrims staying that night. A ferocious thunderstorm that had threatened us on our journey—all of us racing against the purple sky—finally caught up to us and cocooned us in the small space for most of the afternoon.

JV, a kind and gentle francophone from Quebec, treated us to "I Can't Help Falling in Love with You" on guitar, with Marta from Belgium singing it softly in French, while I lay in my bunk, under my blanket, looking out at the storm, enveloped in their sweet lullaby. Listening to the torrential downpour on the roof all afternoon and evening while we filled up on the delicious chickpea stew and conversation by candlelight, we were not surprised or bothered by pots collecting water from the leaky roof—we were sleeping in ruins, after all, amongst family.

The following night passed in Ermita de San Nicolas, a tiny old hermitage built in the thirteenth century, where I bumped into Frankie again. It was a short walk, but one of my favorite stretches of the Way, and it gave me time to linger in the La *Casa de Silencio* (House of Silence) in Castrojeriz. A man named Mau (who looks a lot like what I imagine Rumi would look like roaming around in his flowing garb and long hair), created this space, also called the Temple of Peace, formerly the Hospital of the Soul, as a place for quiet reflection. Remarkably, it looks like all the other houses on the street you pass on the way, but when you open the door, you enter another world, greeted with wafting incense and soft music and a deep sense of stillness. Each room has a space to sit, including the garden in the back (which also has a meditation cave). I learned that he and his partner Nela are building a home just behind San Anton, where I slept the night before. In fact, I believe I saw him talking quite intimately to a tree beside our courtyard yesterday. That whole scene made all kinds of sense now.

I did not rush myself out of the temple and yet had loads of time to get up and over the embankment that rises out of Castrojeriz, to enjoy that singular, sweeping view as you stand on the top, the road before you an undulating ribbon. After committing what was before my eyes to my heart, I made my way slowly down the winding road to find San Nicolas.

What I found on the way was Julie's spirit.

The Littlest Birds

From a taverna in Itero de la Vega, Spain,

Blog Excerpt. September

Day three of the Meseta, that endless plateau, with over two hundred kilometers of what is often described as a boring, empty landscape, with nowhere for the eyes to rest but way out at the far reach of the hay fields. Walking and walking, day after day, toward the ever-distant horizon. It is said the Meseta is where you meet your mind on the Camino and meeting the mind may be another reason why so many people avoid it—so many dark corners in the mind. And yet somehow, for me, the Meseta has been an astonishing gift—a beautiful, sweeping, high plains where the wind holds court and I absolutely love it. Knowing that the number of pilgrims decreases significantly on this section, I have been looking forward to some solitude, some meditative walking and yet, I continue to find chatters. Over these last three weeks, I have appreciated and enjoyed the rich conversation so abundant on the Way and yet, I feel that I have some work to do here and it requires some time alone. Not necessarily thinking, but most definitely an absence of chatter. At the first polite opportunity, I excuse myself, pop my earbuds in and power up my happenstance Camino playlist. Not silence, I grant you, but a step on the way to silence.

Ninety percent of the time I prefer to listen to birds, wind, cowbells, the crunch of my footsteps, my thoughts, or other people. But sometimes I feel the desire to drop into a musical interlude, so I purposely downloaded a few things including Oliver Schroer's *Camino*, for exactly this purpose. In over three hundred kilometers, I have not listened to these. Weird, as Oliver Schroer's recording is one of my favorite collections of music at home and I have been listening to it without let-up, as I imagined and prepared for my journey. Instead, I have a Spotify list I listen to, an odd mix, to be sure, but all related to my Camino in some way. One of them is "The Littlest Birds" by the Be Good Tanyas:

> *"Well, I feel like an old hobo, I'm sad and lonesome and blue. I was fair as a summer's day but now the summer days are through. You pass through places, places pass through you, but you carry them with you on the soles of your traveling shoes."*

The lyrics are set to music so delightful it is almost impossible not to sing, smile and skip along; indeed, I do sing it aloud on the trail, swinging my poles around. It is all I can do not to break into dance. I imagine the onlookers thinking, "Wow, this woman hasn't a clue how to use trekking poles."

I was skipping along thus today, through the fields, on my way to San Nicolas, happy and solitary on the Meseta under an expansive blue sky, when my friend Julie appeared. I felt as if she were with me in some real way, her light, playful, mischievous spirit dancing alongside me. Oh, how I wish I could *will* her here.

Julie was my introduction to the Camino inadvertently via Oliver Schroer's *Camino* wafting through her garden many years ago. It was like a musical painting. A gifted musician, Schroer died in 2008, just fifty-two years old, after a battle with leukemia. At the time of his passing, Julie and I worked together on a palliative care floor, she the social worker and me the occupational therapist; we had forged a vibrant friendship. We called ourselves "soul sisters." I remember us sitting in her adorable house in Guelph, in the back garden with her friend, Michael, who had walked the Camino a few times. Julie said she would love to walk it one day and wondered if it appealed to me. Being somewhat sedentary, I could not imagine walking anywhere for that long—never occurred to me that people might enjoy that—but stepping into Oliver's musical painting was certainly tempting. I wanted to see with my own eyes what inspired this beautiful expression.

Time passed. Not nearly enough time.

Her windowless office, the floor covered in utilitarian gray carpet, was essentially the passage between the medical unit and the gym connecting both to the staff loo on the palliative floor and yet she made the humble space feel like an oasis. I wasn't the only one to drop in to have a sob, usually followed by a belly laugh. My god we had the best laughs! I'd be sitting alone at the table where we had morning rounds and she'd be in her wheelie chair at her desk. Something would be said by one of us and the other would have to jump up to shut the door quickly as we burst into laughter. The pair of us could go from heartbreak to side-splitting laughter in the space of a moment. I put it down to a shared talent for seeing the ridiculous in the most unusual situations. I can still see her lift her knee, hit it with her hand and throw her head back, face convulsed with laughter, tears rolling down her rosy cheeks. A pure, infectious delight. It was a challenge to compose ourselves some days.

Many years ago, she had decided to tag along with me on a trip home to Boston, where I grew up and, on the way, we attended a silent retreat weekend at the Insight Meditation Society in Barre, a center for Buddhist studies in western Massachusetts. At breakfast the first morning, I was pouring myself a cup of coffee in the communal kitchen and Julie came breezing in with her long chestnut curls bouncing, changing the charge in the air, as she did everywhere she went, smiling, asking me how I slept, wasn't it a beautiful morning, where are the cups, etc. I am smiling at her, pointing at stuff and it takes her ages, *ages,* to figure out why I am not answering her directly. When it dawns on her, she covers her mouth and starts laughing, then I start laughing and neither of us can breathe for the fit of silent laughter.

Julie was full of the joy I came hoping to restore. It is helpful to remember as I walk, that the spirit we shared in our friendship was mutual—we were both joyful. Both of us were playful and given to laughter and we could sit with palliative patients in their sorrow, as well as tend our own. Having her beside me reminded me. "Joy and Woe are woven fine," as Blake once wrote. Can't have one without the other.

She never did walk the Camino, but she got to Santiago. She had to take a more expeditious route as she was diagnosed with cancer before her fiftieth birthday and was busy with treatments. The day her sister-in-law called to tell me that she had died was one of the most devastating days of my life. You know those days in your life when the world stops spinning? One day a great chasm emerges, seemingly appearing out of thin air and you know nothing will be the same on the other side, yet there is nothing for it but to find a way to cross. We all have those days.

I was sitting in my car, under a tree in Hamilton after a home visit—I can still remember the client I had just visited with advanced Parkinson's, his devoted wife, the side entrance, all etched in my mind. I remember sitting in the car after the visit, holding the phone, feeling like all the air was suddenly gone. How impossible it seemed that this bright light, this vibrant, generous spirit was no more. Impossible. That afternoon I sat in my garden, weeping and unable to move, thinking of her and, though the April sky was a brilliant blue, the violent gusts of wind ripped branches from the trees. Fitting.

I will make my way back down the road now, dislodge myself from this comfortable local taverna where I have nested for the better part of the afternoon to write. Tonight, I will be staying in a famous old monastery she would have loved— Ermita de San Nicolas. No electricity, stone floors and walls, a couple bunk beds, beautiful Italian hosts and their sweet pup, Fiama. I thought of my much missed and beloved friend when

I entered the tiny monastery earlier and thought with a laugh, *Julie and I would get into so much trouble here.* And I thought, how strange and how fitting that this is the day she appeared, like she knew where I was going and she wanted to tag along. Playful, just like Julie.

I love her and I miss her and I am so glad she is visiting me here on this gusty plateau. I hope we will dance again tomorrow.

Mid-Meseta

The Ermita of San Nicolas, a small rectangular building built in the thirteenth century, sits on a rolling plain, nothing but waving grass all around. The day I arrived, the sky was full of puffy white clouds that brightened the yellow of the spent grass waving in the September breeze. The ermita was managed by Italian volunteers, who were beautiful both inside and out; they filled the place with love, laughter, conversation and, of course, a fantastic dinner of spaghetti and wine served again by candlelight. They even bathe your feet (symbolically) up on the old stone altar.

Frankie and I sat on the bench outside the next morning to don our shoes and to say goodbye to the hospitaleros who had made our stay so restful, even singing us awake in the morning. It had been a true refuge for body and soul.

"How far are you going today?" asked Frankie.

"No plans," I said.

"Me neither, just following my nose," he said.

"I am really enjoying this pace, Frankie, like *really* enjoying it, but if I don't kick it up a notch, I won't get to Santiago until December," I said as we set off into the chill of the morning.

"This is a good problem to have," he said smiling, as we set off.

It had been a restful couple of days; not every moment could be great or you'd lose appreciation for them. I probably shouldn't complain about what came next—the Snoring Caboose—but, of course, I did.

I got an early start walking from the Poblacion Caboose the following morning, for obvious reasons, so I arrived at Carrión de los Condes in time for lunch. I checked into Santa Clara monastery and decided against the bunk rooms, opting instead for a simple, private room with terracotta floor tiles, white walls, a window to the courtyard, a cheerful old yellow and blue bedspread and — what gave me the most cheer— a sparkling tub. And there in town, miraculously, given the physical difficulties she was experiencing, I met up with May.

We had dinner in one of the squares and I ordered what had to be my one hundredth Ensalada Rusa of the journey. These ubiquitous potato salads were getting tiresome, but we non-meat eaters must adjust and I read somewhere that a person can exist on nothing but potatoes. I had met some vegan pilgrims along the way and they really struggled, so by comparison, I had it easy.

"How long do you intend to stay?" I asked her while we waited for the *cervezas*.

"I found a physiotherapist, so I am going to see what they can do if I stay four or five days," May said.

"Wow," I said. "That is quite a chunk of time. How does that impact your Santiago plans?"

"A lot," said May. "And Elliot is coming back to meet me for the last hundred kilometers, so I now have a deadline."

"Have you told him about the trouble you are having with your legs?" I asked.

"No," she said, looking sheepish. "Plans have already been made and hotels booked. I don't want to put anyone out. I'll sort it."

"May," I said. "Don't you think he'd want to know?"

I knew her well enough by now to know, there was no arguing with her. So, we appreciated what I assumed would be our last evening as this stopover for therapy would put too much distance between us. After our goodbye, I went straight back to the monastery, passing vaguely interesting diversions and poured myself a hot bath. This tub, however, had no plug, so I had to use a sock (which once it dried, later became a mitten, which even later became a windshield wiper, all an improvement from its initial role, as it was a terrible sock). I added the fragrant mystery powder that may or may not be bath salts and stayed there until the water went cold.

If you haven't picked up on this yet, a tub has become precious to me. There was a whole incredible town outside my door in Carrión de los Condes, but for me, nothing that compared with the delight of a plugless bathtub.

From there I had a transformative walk to Terradillos de los Templarios—a tiny town most remarkable (to me) for Massage Mary, whom you will soon meet.

A Brief Interlude,
brought to you by Trauma...

"Trauma creates a deep chasm in which an anguished
sense of estrangement and solitude take form."
Mark Epstein, *The Trauma of Everyday Life*

This is the way of trauma. Seems to show up out of nowhere, uninvited, disruptive and ruining the fun. Intrusive. Maybe we should pause and address it directly for a moment, as it was the impetus for my journey. I offer you, humbly, only my lived experience of it.

Trauma, which I think of as an injury to the soul or spirit—whatever you like to call the part of you that makes you, you—rewires your brain in a reflexive, self-protective response to injury. Whatever has happened or has been revealed is so devastating, that the body/mind shuts down to protect itself from annihilation and so dissociation is born. Numbing.

Here but not here. Dissociation takes many forms, but the main function is to detach from reality because reality has become unbearable.

This is a useful survival technique and can help you stabilize the system in an emergency, but in the long term it has problems. Trauma shuts you down from yourself and from others, creating a prison of silence and shame, blunting the emotions and the mind. You become trapped, disintegrated, apart from your body.

Eventually you can't feel anything, bad or good. Nothing gets out, nothing gets in. And here we are, trapped in our cave.

The short story is you can't live that way. Not really.

Occasionally, something slips past the defences and you are drenched in joy. It is so visceral and so fleeting—an excruciating reminder of what you have been missing for so long.

A reminder that something is out there. Outside the cave you retreated to long ago, when all the lights went out.

That is the whisper to wake up.

Something About Mary and Meseta Magic

On the Meseta with all the dearly departed

September 26th over halfway to Santiago

Mary, a local massage therapist, offered treatments at the albergue in Terradillos de los Templarios and what a gift she was. There had been a massage therapist ten kilometers back when my legs were beginning to feel like the bones were splintering inside my flesh, but I didn't stop. I'm not patting myself on the back for fortitude, mind you, I continued because of the pervasive fear of the Completo (full) sign outside the hostel.

Did all these pilgrims not get the memo that everyone skips the Meseta? What were they all doing here?

If I had stopped for that massage earlier—and I did pause to entertain the idea—I would likely not have a bed here in Terradillos because I got the second last bunk and I arrived at one-thirty.

Madness.

I had been doing my best to stay in the present as I walked, trusting that I would get what I needed (as that is a main Camino lesson and proved true at every turn), but the pain in my legs was so bad some days the idea of walking another step was completely unthinkable. In places where there weren't many options, the perceived lack led to anxiety, which likely made the pain worse.

So, I was very glad to be there, particularly with Mary. The music was playing, the incense was going, I whipped off most of my clothes and dove under the sheet.

"Fuerte?" Mary asked as she lay a thick, warm blanket on me.

Ah, a warm blanket; the sweetness of being tucked in.

"Si, si! Muy fuerte," I said enthusiastically.

Being limited in my Spanish and I couldn't say "Dig in sister," so this would have to do. She nodded and we had an understanding.

I pointed at my blisters, my heels and my legs trying to show her the problem points. She must have thought this hilarious, like every pilgrim doesn't come in and say, "Just the feet and legs."

She is having none of it and explains to me, *"Todos,"* with a waving motion over my whole blanketed body.

"Vale," I said. "OK."

She took a bit of time rolling the blanket down my back and stuffing it into my Bridget Jones, OMG those are enormous, flag-like, orange-striped, special hiking underwear* and then dug her strong fingers into my back. I could hear and feel the vertebrae cracking one by one. Painful, but so good at the same time, so good that I was moaning.

She asked me if she should lighten up.

Absolutely not, Mary. Absolutely not.

Was I ever grateful for this woman, her skills and her strong hands. Barely able to walk when I arrived and I was almost fully functional when I rose from the table. Gave her a big hug when I left. It would have been nice to have had a bit of a glute massage as well, but she probably couldn't find them in the enormous orange underpants. You couldn't blame her, really.

I had walked into Carrión de los Condes the previous day with a woman who kept talking about getting the bus to León to shave off some kilometers, but we split up, likely because I had spent most of the evening in that glorious tub. Quite frankly, I was happy to be free of her. That may sound unkind, but I needed to be alone to do some work and this chatter about getting the bus was very tempting, I will not lie. Especially given my painful feet. They were starting to worry me.

---

*The camino group that helped me prepare mentioned that having an unusual color would help you distinguish your underthings on the clotheslines. And while it was proving to be true—no one was mistaking this underwear—I did come to regret going a bit overboard.

How long could this possibly go on, this walking like Frankenstein?

Something was surfacing, like a dormant awareness rising to consciousness, the conditions finally right for it to arise. Doesn't look like much from the outside, but lots of work is happening on the inside. Creating space and cultivating a clear state of mind allows us to see more clearly.

You need some degree of stillness for all this bubbling up. I needed my feet and legs, not because I was interested in a physical accomplishment, but because I needed this simplicity of walking here on the Camino, to allow space for emotional and spiritual healing to occur. In this way, Mary had been tremendously helpful in my journey.

As was the sudden departure of Kevin the day before.

. . .

What happened on the way to meet Mary?

Well, as always, getting lost on the way out of Carrión, I met someone and we walked together for a while. Kevin from Australia was a quick step, but he was interesting and I enjoyed the conversation, so I kept up.

Anyway, suddenly an hour had gone flying past when Kevin had to stop to pee behind a spindly and solitary tree and we agreed to meet down the road for a coffee, but we got separated, permanently. As much as I enjoyed the chat with Kevin, I did not regret our paths diverging because almost as soon as he left, something astounding happened.

First, I should thank Tom Petty. I had added "American Girl" to my happenstance Camino playlist along with the Pretenders, "Stop your Sobbing," and a couple other songs with big energy. With my companion attending to nature's call, I popped in the earbuds and hit the road.

The dirt path is straight as an arrow, fields on either side, nothing but two coffee stops for seventeen kilometers, part of the Meseta that people talk about avoiding. Expansive gray skies and huge spent sunflower fields, rolling fields and stacks of hay bales. Nothing particularly transfixing, but beautiful in a way of its own. Vast, like you are walking in the sky. My feet seemed to have a mind of their own and I could not slow down. I did not want to slow down.

In fact, I walked faster, which surprised me.

I turned the music up and I grew taller, like a string was pulling me up from the heavens. My stride lengthened and I stepped lighter and faster. A thought occurred to me: *I'm not taking the damn bus.* I don't need to take a bus. I don't even want to take a bus.

Suddenly my father was beside me, with such a strong presence I was surprised not to see his shadow next to mine. I could feel him walking with me, remembering him after he developed Parkinson's disease when he used to love walking with music in his ears—the music restoring his confident, quick step, well before the research connected the benefit. His old advice in my head, "If you walk like you know where you are going, no one will stop you." I laughed out loud—all alone except the spirit of my long dead father by my side. *I feel so strong!* Maybe this was more of a mental game than I realized and perhaps my feet hurt because I had been walking off my stride—too slowly. Too much leaning into these damn poles. I started dancing with the poles again, joining them together and swinging them above my head. Raising everything up, opening everything up. Up, up, up! And laughing into the wind.

Out of nowhere and with absolutely no directed effort, I had returned from some long absence—so completely and thoroughly returned.

So much presence in the Meseta. Like the Pyrenees. You just step into it, drop into it. Like it has been waiting patiently for you to show up. Like a threshold waiting only for you to cross it. I had not been sure I would make it to Santiago until this day. Now I feel certain because I am not alone here.

I began to understand all the ways I was not alone. On that second day, it was being seen and connected to Divine spirit, to nature, to the animals that surround me and to beauty. To all of it. Understanding that nothing is separate. Throughout the journey, I have seen and felt the connection between pilgrims, often strangers.

In the Meseta, I felt accompanied in a different way, not alone because I have my ancestors with me, especially my good father, who was so dear to me. When I think of him, I can still feel his hand in mine on his last day as he was dying. He was not conscious, but I felt him in the room, so I talked to him as I held his hand and watched his generous ribcage rise and fall. He had shrunk in the weeks before he died, unable to eat, but his rib cage was as before and reminded me of his size and his strength. Even when his heart and his breath stopped, his great spirit filled the room, though technically deceased. I stood guard to be sure he wasn't alone as family drifted in and out of the bedroom to say goodbye. His spirit stayed the three hours it took my brother Stephen to get there. I left the room so they could have a private goodbye. He was only in there five minutes, but when I went back in after him, the room, which felt full of my father's presence until my brother entered, was empty of spirit and the tree outside the open window had suddenly filled with crows. The crows stayed there in that tree from the night he died until the day of his funeral five days later. When we arrived back to the house after the funeral, they were gone. They never returned.

This is a strong spirit. I knew I was lucky to have him with me even still, though now as a shadow to remind me that I am also strong. I'd just forgotten.

I am strong and I am not alone.

Once again, I was returned to myself, reunited with my spirit, but in a different way. This time with strength and humor, a joining force of ancestors and a thorough and complete letting go of all accounts for harm done by others. Even though what had happened was unforgivable, my attachment to it fell away from me like a petal dropping from my hand, effortless and sweet, which felt different from forgiveness. Compared with the magnificence I was striding into, it was meaningless. I was discarding completely unnecessary baggage, baggage that had weighed so heavily on me these last four years it had stolen my voice and crippled my spirit.

In touch with the higher order of the Universe—Love—the old thief was powerless. I let out a whoop that came right from the earth and up through my feet.

I grew lighter, happier and stronger as I walked into the beginnings of a deeply embodied understanding. I realized that strength must come before letting go, that there is a difference between knowing and being, and that a reliable route to all this wisdom was through the body, bypassing the mind.

Step by step, I felt my spirit walking back into my own skin and bones.

Re-membering myself.

Strong, happy, sure and full of love; I had dead ancestors walking with me. I'd say nothing could stop me now, but without Mary, my seized-up body would not have been able to continue the following day to Bercianos. Turns out that no matter how strong we are, we all need each other; what a good thing that is.

To Mary, my dad, my dearly departed, all those who had helped me get this far, Tom Petty and all the glorious magic that is the Meseta...deepest bows of gratitude.

End of the Meseta
to the Cantabrian Foothills

The donativo in Bercianos was nearly impossible to find. Wandering through the nearly desolate town that had been built like a maze, hot dust caking my skin, the end of an already long walk became another nearly unbearable and sloppy stumble, but it was well worth my determined search. The kind owners at Bar El Sueve got me around the final corner and there was a man standing on the steps of a beautiful stone building, smiling at me and waving. I turned around to see if there was someone behind me.

Nope. Just me.

"*Tú*," the man exclaimed in my general direction. "*Te hemos estado esperando!*"

When I looked confused, the man who I would come to know as Gustav, said, "Peregrina, we have been waiting for you!"

He took my bag, ushered me in and poured me a glass of lemon water. I felt so welcomed—an honoured guest. My goodness, couldn't we all do this for each other more of the time?

The Bercianos *hospitaleros,* Gustav and his companion Angel, were like a pair of loving, hilarious uncles. When I handed Angel my passport, he regarded my photo taken nine years ago with my dark hair and relatively youthful face.

He held up my passport and said, "This woman is beautiful."

Then he put it down, took my hand in his and before I could make any self-deprecating remarks about my now white hair—it had been a challenging decade—he said, squeezing my hand, "But this woman, wow, beautiful *y muy, muy interesante.*"

What a sweetheart. And it remained sweet even after I heard him say something very similar to a pilgrim who came in later that day. Just a couple fellas trying to make weary, sweaty people feel good and isn't that lovely.

Many of us helped to prepare the salad for dinner, set the tables and pour the wine. These accumulating donativo experiences had me excited about volunteering myself one day, to offer this kind of welcome to others. Bercianos has a famous dinner blessing rap, which involves chanting, clapping and smacking the long table in unison. Gustav did a great job leading the other thirty pilgrims in the dining hall—a happy cacophony of the best sort.

After our shared meal, Angel herded us out to the rocks behind the refuge to pay homage to the sun as it settled into the hills in the distance. This is getting to be an enjoyable habit and stopping to acknowledge the sun doing its thing is even more enjoyable in community. Angel grabbed my phone and took a selfie with me and the other dozen pilgrims who congregated. Later, I would find a special someone was with me that evening because she would find herself in this photo, sitting quietly on a rock behind me, eyes closed, smiling at the world.

A gift yet to be born.

Before retreating to my bunk, I wandered over to the local bar around the corner to use the Wi-Fi and looked up the bus schedule to León. Just in case. There's no harm in collecting information, is there? I was surprised to see a bus to León did in fact leave from this tiny village, but, of course, never on a Thursday, so this being Wednesday, there was no decision to be made. Not today anyway.

The following evening, in a tiny town called Reliegos, I luxuriated in a sprawling room that could easily fit a few more of me, a room I pre-booked in a panic yesterday when I was advised all the beds were full between Bercianos and León. Turns out it was fake news, but it is fake news that gets attention when your legs are aching. It was a quiet place and the mother and daughter who operated it were sweet. It was a perfect spot to collect my thoughts and think about the days ahead—León and beyond. I did not have much interest in León, outside the gorgeous cathedral and the Gaudi building.

It seemed the longer I walked in this way, the less tolerance I had for busy city energy.

Frankie showed up in a fine spirit with a few friends while I was sitting outside on the patio and we caught up over a beer and snacks. This man made me laugh every time. A good soul with a great sense of humor and no pretense. They were hoping to book the Parador in León for the night but found it closed so were trying to rent a house. I don't know what they eventually decided, but they pushed on and I remained in the tiny town as it grew dark, content in my solitude, watching the street cats hunt along the road.

Judgment, Humility,
and Rosie Takes the Bus
September 30th

One of the many lessons of the Camino is to refrain from judging, even though judging can be rampant here. Rampant. Just the other day, four people looking impossibly clean and sporting linen shorts, passed by on the Way with their colorful, tidy day packs. Frankie, who was resting with me on a bench, laughed and said, "Looks like these guys are headed for the country club."

I thought that seemed harsh and said so, but then the cloud of men's cologne drifted back, nearly choking me. I had to agree with him, "Oh, come on, cologne?"

Normally, I say it is none of my business and I keep doing my own thing. Like when the Irish girl, Queenie, rolled into the albergue in Hornillos a week before with her wheeled purple valise, curly red head held high. She later said that she had agreed to come along to meet her dad on the Camino and he had not explained the particulars (nor did she look them up, to be fair), so she'd had to ship said valise to each stop. She felt a little silly about the whole predicament but wasn't going to give anyone the satisfaction. Good for her.

Then there were the folks carrying suitcases down the rockslide into Zubiri on day three. I almost stopped to ask if they were alright, but I was barely managing to walk myself, so I decided not to get involved with whatever was going on there. My Orisson friends, Elliot and May, later saw the silent couple wheeling the suitcases up to the steel pilgrim sculpture on Alto de Perdon, and when I say up, I mean straight up. Steep path. Big loose rocks. Who knows, maybe they thought they were paying a penance of some sort. Probably overkill, Sisyphus.

None of our business. Just do your own Camino.

If there is any religious judgment here, it seems to be way less than the judgment on bag carrying and albergue staying. I was raised Catholic, with all the sacraments, the catechism lessons (CCD), the nuns, the light dusting of guilt, etc. If I had to pick a team now (not that I think we should have teams because that implies competition and comparison) I would say I am Buddhist, but normally I just say I am atheist. While this is technically true (a-theism, no god), I am sure it gives the wrong impression.

Tricky, this labeling of something so vast.

I had an ex-father-in-law who defined himself as a "practicing" atheist, which was sort of funny, but he was totally serious. I had a dream about him on the walk, which was strange as I hadn't thought of him in ages and he died more than a decade ago. I seem to have a lot of communication with the dead, but I was still hoping for my sister Nancy to turn up.

We all know what judgment is and that we are better off not to participate in it (at least in a personal way), but what about humility? According to Merriam Webster, humility is freedom from pride or arrogance—I like that. In San Nicolas, the volunteers wash the feet of the pilgrims in a symbolic gesture, humbling both the giver and the receiver. It seems to be rooted in a belief that we're all in this together, sometimes you're up and sometimes you're down. It's all OK.

Where am I going with this?

Well, I mostly mention it in relation to my declarations of strength in the Meseta and my bold assertions of not needing any damn bus and I'm going to walk until my feet fall off, powered by the ancestors, etc. Perhaps it is good to remember that some happenings are not meant to be taken quite so literally. Of course, one can be strong and still take a bus from time to time. Not if you are in a race, it should go without saying, especially with prize money attached, that is illegal.

Rosie Ruiz became infamous when she won the first-place female runner in the Boston marathon and was later found to not have run the whole course. Did she jump out of the crowd toward the end? Perhaps. I wasn't there. That was the judgment anyway. After that controversy, another surfaced regarding some question of her taking the subway for part of the New York City marathon. Look, no one is perfect and we all do things we regret. Ideally, they do not land in the news.

All this to distract you, of course, from the fact that despite my assertions in the Meseta about not needing any damn bus, I bused both in and out of León—in for a penny, in for a pound.

Come on. You had to see that coming.

And all that gained time allowed me to enjoy the garden of Refugio Gaucelmo in Rabanal, where I wrote these notes over some wine and cheese. The skies were blue and my laundry was drying on the line while I reflected on my journey. Two days prior, the day I bussed fifteen kilometers out of León, I restored myself in a vegetarian, yogi albergue delight in Hospital de Órbigo. I walked there with Annie, whom I met on the bus. We both swung in hammocks in the garden, frolicked with puppies, yes, puppies and enjoyed massages because we had extra time and we were happy. So happy.

Should we feel guilty?

No.

When someone said they had injured themselves walking too far, the osteopath who provided the massages shook her head and said, "It is not the purpose of the Camino to suffer."

Amen, sister.

It is not about more suffering. The suffering was the preamble.

I didn't take the bus because I had to. I did it because I wanted to, I decided to love myself and I have zero regrets about this. The road in and out of León is industrial, concrete and sometimes dangerous. I had zero interest in subjecting myself to all that palaver and preferred to keep my bones and ligaments able to walk all of Galicia into Santiago and hopefully, to the sea. If someone wants to walk every step, that's cool, well done. I didn't. I do not regret it now, don't anticipate regretting it later and I am sure God, in whatever form, is not judging me for this.

Roderic and Roderic, the father and son duo from the Cacophony Caboose, who kept turning up telling me I would feel better if I did the whole walk, maybe they have an opinion. Let them. That is not my concern. Those two were literally sitting in the vacant patio under my open window in Reliegos at nine pm the night before I got on the bus in Mansilla de las Mulas, craning their necks to wish me a good night and to tell me that the bus did not exist. A truly bizarre moment.

For the record, I had a lot of fun on the bus with the ten other wayward pilgrims watching the path roll by at record speed and was so delighted that I was not walking for a change. So, here's to living our own lives, minding our own business, walking our own Caminos and not caring what anyone else thinks of it.

Tomorrow I am walking to la Cruz de Ferro (the Iron cross) for sunrise, the place people put the stones they carry from home to symbolize the burden they would like to put down, or something they wish to release. I did not bring a stone and I do not regret that either. I have been littering the Camino with my old burdens from as early as the second day. I like the symbolism, but I already carry too much and have no need of a stone, as my heart has been full of them for years.

But that is just my Camino.

Stolen Voices

Let's talk about Imposter Syndrome

It is a bit of a quandary. This idea of voice and ownership.

Is it my story to tell? What part is mine to tell?

All the ways our voices are silenced.

One of the biggest ones, at least in this story, is feeling like a fraud. Can I be traumatized if I've stepped into Joy and am having a little fun? Of course I can. But with extended periods of gaslighting, the question of others' perceptions hangs around like a ghoul. Can I be alienated even if I'm in occasional contact with the person from whom I am alienated? Yes, especially when nearly every interaction feels like a flopped audition for a role I thought I already had and the relationship itself is decimated.

Maybe I was just a horrible mother.

In creeps doubt and a gnawing sense that my identity as a parent is in question, not just by others, but eventually by my own doubts and insecurities. That is probably the worst, when you start to forget who you are. You begin to gaslight and erase yourself—it is a lot less work for everyone else.

This doesn't happen overnight, but the longer you are told you don't matter, that you are without worth, that your pain doesn't matter, the more you start to believe it. Your internal voice starts to change.

I don't deserve to be heard.

These thoughts are compounded by the manipulation and distortion of reality often involved in familial alienation, where your intentions and actions are constantly misinterpreted or twisted by others. Your reality is erased. You begin to feel invisible, and the more you try to reach out, to assert your presence, the more you are pushed back. With that distance grows the sense of alienation from yourself.

You begin to doubt the authenticity of your love, your worth and your role as a parent. The fear that you will never be enough—that no matter what you do, it's not enough to undo the damage—is relentless. And yet, amidst it all, there's a fragile hope: somehow, someday, you will find a way back and your child will come to see you for the person you've always been, not the distorted version generated by others. It is no wonder there is a correlation between alienation and severe psychological distress, both for the parent and the child.

Even more difficult to talk about, but necessary, is imposter syndrome in the context of suicidal feelings. This creates a haunting sense of disconnection from one's own pain. It's as if you're trapped in a space between feeling like you don't belong in the world—believing that your struggles are either not valid or are too much for others to understand—and yet never crossing the line into actually ending your life—thankfully. It's the paradox of wanting to feel better, but also not wanting anyone to know that you need help. Feeling unworthy of help. If you have been told for some time that you are not worthy of basic respect, that feeling makes sense. It isn't true, but it makes sense one would feel that way.

You become an outsider in your own life, questioning why you're still here when everything feels like it's falling apart. You're stuck in limbo, feeling like a fraud in your own existence, wrestling with worthlessness and wondering if you deserve the help you so desperately need, let alone the life you're barely holding on to.

I lost her. Then I lost myself.

Ever since, I have been existing in a life suspended, neither alive nor dead.

. . .

The Camino, as difficult as it could be, was nothing compared to trying to live a life half-dead, for years trying to live when there was nothing left to live for, hope imploding. When I set out, I hoped the Camino would be my bridge back to the land of the living. When I set out, I was just grasping at straws, trying to stay afloat long enough for something to shift. And there had been many shifts already, through moments of Grace as early as the second day. I have been given so much. I honestly thought the gifts were finished.

Wrong again, Pilgrim.

INTO THE MISTS

(Galicia)

Six Days to Santiago

Along with the ubiquitous rocks in the road, I don't recall Camino veterans mentioning panic attacks as the 100km mark approaches.

There have been many days when I absolutely *love* the idea of returning to regular life, where there is an exciting selection of shoes waiting for me (once the swelling goes down) and where I can go longer than two days before my clean under things run out. Oh, to enjoy the freedom to leave the house for the day and not have to pack up all my things, paranoid I've left something behind and relocate before nightfall, just to repeat the whole process in the morning. Why wouldn't I want to return to a life without blisters, without Compeed plasters or foot greasing, without daily discomfort and pain and without smelling my clothes to see if they are clean. Oh, to return to a place where I can shower without flip flops, use a fresh, thick towel instead of my sarong and always have a dry place to put my things down.

Sheets! Such luxuries.

And I'm not telling you the half of it. We all walked through cow shit the other day and while of course, you avoid the obvious patties when you can, what with all the rain and mud running down the road, there really was no telling what you were stepping in and all around was the fresh scent of early morning farm. You just get used to these things and get on with it. (No, I am not bringing my shoes home.)

Later that same afternoon, a kind woman shared her hairdryer with me and another pilgrim, and what a treat it was not to have to walk around in the cold with wet hair for a change. Unfortunately, we had been so long without, neither of us really remembered how to use one properly and though we were dry and significantly more comfortable, by the time we finished we looked like we walked off the set of a 1960's beach flick. It was ridiculous paired with our Camino gear, but we were dry and had a good laugh.

I suspect what is giving rise to the panic, something the promise of reunification with life's little luxuries cannot quell, is something mentioned in the first verse of *A Pilgrim's Prayer* by Fraydino. "Although I may have traveled all the roads, crossed mountains and valleys from east to west, if I have not discovered the freedom to be myself, I have arrived nowhere." It goes on to remind us of all the ways we have grown, all the blessings we have bestowed and have received, and all of it is for nothing if we don't bring it home. Really bring it home.

People think it is hard to walk eight hundred kilometers, but once you get to the beginning (which *is* hard), it is just one step in front of the other, surrounded by sweet people who are ready to help when you are down. You do what you can, as long as you can and you just keep moving forward. No creature comforts, sure, but straightforward as far as these things go and a life this simplified can be quite enjoyable. In terms of fear of getting horribly lost, a fear I am familiar with, there are maps and apps and signs all over the roads.

It is difficult to go too far wrong.

No, walking is not so hard. Painful at times, but not hard.

What is hard is changing my life. Making myself vulnerable. Going back and, despite the discomfort, making the changes that I have been avoiding, dancing around them because I want there to be some other way. A way that isn't full of loss and sadness and difficult choices. I want to continue to "wait and see" because then I can avoid the hard truths. And none of this change would be necessary if I hadn't walked all this way to see behind the veil. To feel the joy of life in my bones, appreciate the beauty of everything and feel the depth of love all around me, and really, really understand what a truly precious gift our time here is.

The difficult work is that once I know how I want my life to look, it is my responsibility to create it. No maps, no ready-made support group and no yellow arrows left on rocks or posts to show the way. Sure, there are signs, but they are much more difficult to spot.

My friend JV rubs his belly and says, "You must check here when you decide something. How does it feel?"

He is right. The body knows. Quiet the mind and your body will not steer you wrong.

OK, but arrows would be easier.

It has not been an easy time. Somehow, I anticipated walking into the mists of Galicia would bring a nice soft landing—Van Morrison playing in my ears, smiles, only days to the finish line. Silly, presumptuous me believed it would be soft because many people talk about Galicia being the spiritual part of your journey, where you meet spirit, like the Meseta and the mind and I thought I was well in touch with my spirit, so I was expecting something familiar and gentle. Some reflection. Maybe some meditation.

Well didn't I get the shock of my life. I was humbled and grateful, it's just that I really didn't expect Galicia to be the hardest of all.

A Horse on the Way and Other Blessings
Somewhere in Galicia

(This began some days back and finishes some days hence. Time is different in Galicia. Well, time is always different, we just accept this in Galicia.)

The road up to O Cebreiro is steep and long and, as much as I love to climb, when I heard there was a guy with horses at the base, I was all over that option. Somehow, I had the notion that you just saunter up and hire a horse. Wasn't that ridiculous? I know, but on the Way, I have become used to following a serendipitous, "if it was meant to be" sort of philosophy and, barring a couple stunning fails, it has worked out beautifully almost all the time. But I was attached to the idea of the horse, so I put a bit of effort in and found out I had to arrange to ship my backpack and make a reservation for an afternoon because his morning trips were reserved out for days.

Committed as I was, I arranged two whole days at the last minute around my reservation for an afternoon horse, a little more complicated, but doable. The walk to Molinaseca from Rabanal nearly did me in (someone broke their leg the day before on the slippery, wet shale), but I made it to Cacabelos, which is where I bumped into JV again. We had dinner, the usual fare, but it was so nice to chat with him, as always. I saw him the day before at the Iron Cross, obviously sitting with some deep sadness, so I left him to his reflections and continued to Molinaseca where I hatched the plan for the horse. I told JV over dinner what I was up to.

"You take a horse? Why?" he asked between bites of his pilgrim meal, his blue eyes sparkling with his usual curiosity.

"I don't know, I read about it somewhere and it sounds like fun. You want to come?" I asked.

JV threw his head back laughing, "Me? No. I walk. Why I walk from Italy then take the horse?"

He thought it was hilarious. My Quebecois amigo was going every step. I wouldn't see him again until Santiago.

In order to make this horse dream a reality, I had a forty-kilometer day in front of me, which is basically two days of travel in one for me at my current rate of speed with the bi-lateral Achilles tendonitis (diagnosed in Refugio Gaucelmo's garden in Rabanal by a Canadian physiotherapist, the day before the Iron Cross), but nearly six kilometers were on a horse so she gets some of the credit. Mind you, I did pitch myself on this horse at three pm after walking from seven in the morning with only one quick break and, when I managed a graceless dismount at five pm at the top of the mountain, my right leg was numb, making for a scary landing, so my body was a full participant for the entire journey (unlike the bus scandal, which I never did come to regret).

O Cebreiro is the gateway to Galicia on the Camino Francés and many say a place of great spiritual importance. An ancient church sits atop the mountain—a simple building set back from the road. Rumour had it that there was a devoted priest there who said a Pilgrim Mass every night, followed by a beautiful blessing—it was not to be missed. As it turned out, I would indeed miss it on account of all the rooms in the tiny village having been reserved well in advance. Other than this horse adventure, I have been mostly living in the moment, and had come to find it an important part of the healing process. Yesterday, after booking the horse, I reserved a bed in the village past O Cebreiro, Liñares, but I arranged for my pack to be delivered here, to O Cebreiro, just in case a vacancy came up.

It did not.

The horse handler said it was a twenty-minute walk to Liñares, no worries, so I wandered around to get the circulation back in my bottom half, enjoyed the view over a glass of wine with some new friends and finally called the hostel, which is when I found out I was barely going to make it in time before the person locked up for the night. This tidbit of information turned my last four kilometers into a lumbering jog, alone, through the woods, with a backpack weighing fifteen pounds or more—something I don't recommend.

And of course, because I was rushing, I fell. A mess.

It was quite a full day.

The horse turned out to be a mixed blessing, not that I'm complaining. I just find it fascinating that so often the things we anticipate with high expectations fall short and the real stunners come right out of the clear blue sky. The horse taking most of the work out of the climb was an absolute treat and I do love being around animals, so my time with Brisa was special.

However, Brisa was a nibbler and needed to be redirected from grazing the hillside, quite often actually. For the first hour, this wasn't a big problem, but towards the end of the two hours, I just didn't have the strength. To be honest, I think she took a bit of advantage. The numbness in my leg resolved eventually, so that wasn't a big deal. The views were gorgeous, magical really, and I have no photos of course, as I was riding a horse I could barely manage. In the end, the biggest issue was that I just was not convinced the horses were enjoying this way of life, up and down the mountain, day after day and it all felt a bit tainted because of this. Don't think I'd do it again.

Moreover, to arrive on time, I really had to hustle, which meant no rest breaks, no stretching and somehow, I flew right past beautiful Villafranca del Bierzo without seeing it and the same goes for Trabadelo. I remember nothing from these places, I was moving that fast. Along the way, I bumped into a group of American women who I had been leapfrogging with for about a week. They usually moved a bit faster than me, so we only saw each other at rest stops. This time I was on fire, so I ended up walking with them for a half hour or so. When the cat lover amongst them stopped to feed her followers for the second time, I kept moving. Nancy, the fastest of the bunch, walked with me for a bit and told me the story of why she was there. Our conversation deepened when I asked why her husband was not walking with her, seeing as he had planned out the entire walk with all the stops, places of interest, etc.

I was just getting ready to launch into the "Well, he's got a nerve," bit, when she told me that he died at the end of last year. (Again, never miss an opportunity to keep your mouth shut.) He knew he was dying and had planned the walk to help her cope with the grief. All these women had volunteered to walk along with her to support her. We talked a while more, a tender and open-hearted conversation about what her husband meant to her and how the support of these women, and the Camino itself, were indeed helping her heal and we suddenly found ourselves in the ancient chestnut grove, just before

Trabadelo. We stopped while she read the history of how these trees had sustained so many through famines. She wanted to wait for her friends to catch up, so they didn't miss the grove, but I needed to keep moving due to my date with a horse, so we said goodbye and I started off.

"Wait, I want you to have this," she said.

I turned back to her. She took a bracelet with a silver shell off her wrist and slipped it on mine and told me she had meant to give this to me if she saw me again, to make me an honorary Camino Sister, along with the friends she was walking with and women she felt a special connection with on her journey. We both had tears and we hugged each other before going our own ways. There are no words for what this connection meant to me and it wouldn't have happened if I hadn't been rushing for a horse.

Later that day, when I arrived at the one hostel town eight minutes before they locked the door, after nearly breaking my leg outside O Cebreiro, I heard familiar voices coming from the kitchen and poked my head inside. It was four Australians I had met way back in Pamplona and lost touch with because they were speedy and I had lingered self-indulgently for days in my Burgos bathtub. Last time I saw them we were walking through a park, weeks ago, talking about bladder infections (story for another time). They all seemed so happy in each other's company, it was a delight to be near them—even after they showed me their questionable bug bites. I was so happy to see them and it was such a surprise. For sure it made me happier than the horse.

Because I had injured myself sliding into home base with eight minutes to spare that night, I decided I needed an easy next day and planned to stop in a little place I would have normally pushed past. The little stop, Filloval, just outside Triacastela was most remarkable for the bar which made the best vegetarian food I had had in a month. Lentil soup. These moments sound simple, but I remember every spoonful.

As delightful as that was, I had one more blessing to come. Once again, inside the little hostel that was neither here nor there, as I was scoping out the laundry situation, I heard a familiar, lilting voice and turned.

"Bridget?" I asked, not believing it possible.

She turned from where she was sitting at the registration table to look up, surprised to hear her name, perhaps. I couldn't believe it—it was her. I hadn't seen her since the morning of August 31st when she started her walk, the day before mine. I loved her mystical Celtic energy when we shared a group dinner on my first night in Saint-Jean-Pied-de-Port and I had thought of her off and on throughout my month walking, hoping we would meet again, but thinking it not at all likely. What a Camino gift, my Irish friend appearing just inside Galicia's doorstep, how absolutely fitting.

We spent the rest of the afternoon and evening catching up on all our stories from the road, re-learning how to use a hairdryer, sharing a great meal with new friends and watching the sunset. Dinner companions included Vivi from Denmark (Bridget's friend from the Way who I would also come to love), Helen from Italy who had kindly shared the hairdryer and was carrying more emotional luggage than she at first seemed, Kama from the United States, the best of America—inclusive, kind and friendly to the extreme. Laughing, sharing, crying; sharing the weight and sharing the joy. I felt like I had found a few members of my long-lost family.

Three of us would spend the next four days traveling together and all these women would become dear to me. I had become convinced now, toward the end of this walk, that everyone is beautiful when you really see them. Love for all becomes second nature when you begin to see with your heart and once we can let ourselves be seen, which can take some time.

Vivi

We set out from Filloval, together, down into the valley into Triacastela and chose the road that passes Samos to visit the old monastery there. It was a beautiful trail, through dense woodland, past fields of grazing cows and falling down wooden gates. We walked in easy silence and occasional chatter. Once or twice, Bridget would stop to "download" a poem (she meant from an unseen muse) and Vivi and I would amble on. She had such a happy, sweet spirit. We talked about many things, including a bit about life at home.

Vivi described her life back in northern Denmark with an obvious fondness; she spoke warmly of her grown children, her partner and her dog. It sounded deliciously full to me.

"Oh yes," she said, "We are very lucky, I know. Of course nothing is perfect."

"Of course," I said.

"We struggle with all the same things; who does the dishes, who walks the dog. But we always end up laughing," she said smiling, with a wistful look. "Nothing is so serious."

It sounded like exactly what I wanted in my life—a gentle fullness and love. The night we met in Filloval, she had popped outside to talk to her partner Rob on WhatsApp and I didn't hear the conversation, but I could see her whole face lit up.

We rounded the corner to Samos, an enormous monastery in the middle of the woods, excited to see the albergue. For all the glamor of the main part of the building, the albergue out back was dismal and pilgrims do not have high standards at this point in the walk, so that is saying something. As we were checking in, the monk (Brother Fred) at the simple desk in front asked us how we arrived.

"Did you travel by foot, or by bike?" he inquired.

"By foot," said Vivi, answering for all of us.

"Actually, she travels by horse," said Bridget, smirking and pointing at me.

He looked confused, "I am afraid we don't have facilities for a horse."

"It's OK, I left him in O Cebreiro," I said, giving Bridget a look.

"You left your horse?" Now he seemed alarmed.

Bridget walked away laughing, leaving me to explain that I really am arriving by foot and I have not abandoned an animal mid-Camino.

Brother Fred was a student at the monastery. He was maybe in his late thirties, and apparently had little in the way of company or conversation here. After we resolved the "mode of transportation" requirements, he bent our ears for a half hour before giving us the go ahead to grab a bunk in the deserted hall. I gathered from the nature of his depressed chatter that he was not enjoying himself in his post.

I certainly hope his accommodations were better than these dimly lit green plaster walls, dotted with mold. It was a bit like the horse in that there was much anticipation to arrive here, but the bald reality fell short. We didn't spend much time in our cell, as you might imagine, but after visiting the monastery, there were not many other places to go so we hung about on benches, as pilgrims do. Bridget pulled out her *credencial* to see if we'd been to any of the same albergues.

"Did you stay in this one," she asked us. "The hippy place with the hammocks?'

"Oh," I said, "I know what you mean. They had geese running around. One of them was a little nippy."

"Yes, that's the one. Great place. The woman was singing and playing guitar after dinner."

"Oh, nice. It was too early in the day for me to stay when I got there, so I missed all that. I just stopped for coffee. But the geese were a riot." I flipped through my pages and found my Bercianos stamp. "Did you stop here? It was near the end of the Meseta."

Vivi looked over, "Oh yes, I was there. Beautiful sunset."

She looked at her stamp and compared it to mine. She gasped and started laughing, "Same day! The funny hospitalero made a picture, remember?"

I pulled out my phone, scrolled backwards in time and, sure enough, there was Vivi,

Sitting peacefully on a rock, eyes closed, smiling at the sun.

"So, near all along," I said.

The three of us were parked outside on the bench when Vivi got a video call from her partner, Rob, so we got to meet him briefly. He was throwing a birthday party for Vivi's daughter (they are a beautifully blended family—he has two children, she has two children) and there was some family joke about the kind of apple cake he made—lots of laughter and smiling, clearly loads of affection all around. It was touching, but wow, did it hurt.

This was so far from what my life had become and, if it hadn't been sweet Vivi, I think I may have felt pangs of jealousy. Instead, I felt longing and a recognition—a deep awareness of what I was missing. It was a lesson; in fact, it was one of the most important lessons of the whole journey and was a catalyst to everything that happened when I returned.

Those misty days in Galicia, though often challenging, were an exceptional gift. Interesting that though Brisa the horse ended up playing only a minor role, the whole end of my journey may have been radically different if I hadn't been hurrying to make the horse deadline.

As time went on and the mist deepened, I found it extraordinary that the harder I tried to make a plan, the more expeditiously the Universe would crumple it up and toss it away like an old receipt.

Amenal. Fifteen kilometers left.

I can't believe it. And the final morning walk will be through a forest in the dark. Another birth canal, like the forest that deposited me in Roncesvalles.

Arriving. Part One.

Santiago

The morning I walked into Santiago, I started in the dark forest, alone, for absolutely no good reason, which was silly because I did not even intend to get the *compostela* until the following day, on the anniversary of my father's death. And I had a delightful hotel booked as a treat for myself, so there was absolutely no need to rush for a bed. Bridget and Vivi had slowed down a few days back and I pushed forward, feeling worried that I might not make it on the twelfth and here I was, a day early. Rushing seemed to be something forty days had not corrected.

On my way that morning, thinking (erroneously) that this would be my last day of walking, I intentionally left one pole at the base of a hill in case someone needed it. Then I left the other one behind in a cafe by mistake, so the last eight kilometers were without external physical support. Once again, doesn't sound like much, yet I can tell you, it is shocking what a difference poles make. The adrenalin of nearly finishing carried me most of the way until I got to the edge of the city, which went on forever, then I felt like my legs were broken again.

Mental game, girl, it's a mental game.

Limping my way forward across the bridge that connected me to the city, I thought: *Funny, alone leaving Saint-Jean-Pied-de-Port on day one and alone again at the other end arriving in Santiago.* Yet, I was almost never alone in between. Just like life—we are born alone and we die alone. As I think about birth and death in relation to my Camino, now that I am on the other side of it (the Camino, that is), it occurs to me that leaving Saint-Jean-Pied-de-Port was a death of the old self, the old way of life and the arrival in Santiago (or Finisterre or Muxía) was a birth and a beginning. I say it occurs to me, but I know the Camino is a metaphor and there are many who have come before who have had similar thoughts. The forty days in between did very much feel like a womb and I felt a mixture of excitement and trepidation to leave the warmth and safety. But my feet felt only excitement.

I abandoned the arrows and engaged the GPS on my phone, knowing the arrows were often not the most direct route in the cities and my main mission at this point was not to follow the "official" Camino, but to get rid of this fucking backpack and take my shoes off as soon as humanly possible. Because of this, I did not enter through the main gate, past the bagpiper in the archway, which I would have enjoyed had I known he was there, but walked around the back of the cathedral, not even knowing it was the cathedral and up a couple blocks to my hotel.

An understated way to arrive, to be sure.

Funny how underwhelming it can be, arriving in Santiago. Mind you, it was never intended to be my final destination, but arriving is a pretty big deal, regardless. And to be honest, there was a big part of me that was sad that this otherworldly time, this liminal space, was coming to an end. Don't get me wrong, it was nice to be finished and I was pleased that I made it, because there was never any guarantee of that.

After giving all the pertinent check-in details, the kind man at the hotel desk handed me the keys to my room (111) and told me if I hurried, I could make it to the Pilgrims' Mass at noon.

It did seem significant that my room number was 111, I had arrived on the 11th of October and it was 11:11 when I arrived at the hotel. After a bit of a collapse on the bed, I looked that up because it sounded familiar. Apparently, the number 11 is a "master" number. Turns out it represents illumination, the presence of spirit guides and some other powerful things (to numerology folks at least). So, it seemed either I was being welcomed to Santiago by my deceased relatives—and the

following day would be the anniversary of my father's death—
or visited by some other spirit presence. Or it could be I stood
at a portal to my spiritual awakening, at the very threshold of
my true nature and purpose. (Rattled that all off like reading a
fortune cookie but, in truth, none of that sounds kooky to me
after this journey.)

Scanning my room, I made a mental note of the bathtub
for later and shuffled off to the Pilgrim Mass in my flip flops.
Seems like a lot of Masses for an atheist, I grant you, but these
were important rituals of arrival and I could appreciate that
without much inner conflict. Though I have to say, I did prefer
the short ones.

The cathedral was under construction, so it was held
in another smaller church, which was packed—not a great
situation given the shape I was in. I managed to perch on
the corner of a column base, a pointy triangle of cold stone,
using exhausted quads to levitate as much as possible. Can
you feel that delight? Right between the sitting bones. Yeah,
that didn't last long. Some people were sitting on the floor,
but to be honest, I wasn't sure if I was equal to the task of the
contortions required to lower myself down, never mind ever
manage to get up—you know how the Catholic Masses are
up and down, up and down, keeping everyone awake. I didn't
want to chance making a holy show of myself, so I just leaned
fashionably against the column, in a whole lot of discomfort.

I lasted maybe fifteen minutes and thought, enough, and crept down the side aisle and back into the daylight.

It was then I remembered I should probably find the Pilgrim House because my documentation to get back into Canada was (hopefully) mailed there. Fairly important. Most people would have gone there first, but not me. I was just wandering around the town in my flip flops, without a plan and in a bit of a daze.

The manager who had the document locked up somewhere was out, so I made myself a coffee and talked to Joe, one of the volunteers. It was a little slice of home. There was a warm welcome and an invitation to sit and do some reflection, the latter offering I found myself not in the mood for, task-focused as I was in the moment. While he was filling me in on the history of the House, a center that acts as a support for pilgrims entering Santiago, the manager returned.

"Great timing," he said. "This arrived not too long ago, just around eleven this morning."

"What a coincidence," I said, a little freaked out by another eleven. "So did I."

Spirits everywhere.

Documents secured, Mass aborted and now I wondered what else I would do to fill my time. Too early for bath and wine. As I mentioned, the big cathedral was closed for renovations, sadly, but I heard you could get inside to see it via the museum. I walked back behind it, the way I had entered the city and followed a stream of people into a side door. Joining a rather long line up that snaked around the space, I found myself inside the cathedral doors but not in the cathedral proper. In truth, I had no idea where I was, other than maybe almost inside a cathedral. No one spoke English around me, so instead of attempting communication, I decided, lazily, to assume this must be the line for the museum. A good half-hour later, it looked like I was passing through an entrance of some sort, a stone archway.

It's weird there is no charge. I'm pretty sure it cost four euro to get into the museum. Hmm. Maybe it is free on whatever day this is.

We walked single file up the short flight of marble steps. The man in front of me bent to the side and seemed to be hugging some kind of statue. It looked like the back of a head or bust. OK, well it takes all kinds, right? No judgment from me.

I continued to follow this line and we descended some steps to walk past a tiny casket where people were kneeling to pray. Must be someone important, but this is not my thing either, so I walked past that as well. Thinking this is all the preamble to, I don't know, some larger part of the cathedral, the giant, swinging thurible known as the botafumeiro perhaps, which, if I am honest, is all I am really interested in at this point and I am surprised when we are deposited back to where we started.

Well, *that* was a waste of time. It is a good thing it was free.

I wandered back through the town to pick up some wine for the bath because it was that kind of day and, after all, I did just walk across Spain. Coming out of the shop, I heard my name being called.

"Colleen! Is that you?"

Of all the bizarre coincidences, there was George and Diane from the Toronto Camino group waving to me.

"What are you doing here?" I asked after giving them both a big hug.

"We just finished the Portuguese route," said Diane.

"Well actually, we're just back from Muxía this afternoon," said George.

"We wanted to walk, but we're cutting it close on time, so we took the bus," said Diane. "It was phenomenal. If you have time, you might want to add it in."

"Oh, are you heading home soon?" I asked.

"No, we're having a bit of a wander. We have a flight to England tomorrow. George has family there still," said Diane.

"Do you have time for a pint?" asked George.

"All the time in the world," I said.

We grabbed seats at the nearest sunny patio and got caught up on their walk up the coast, my walk across Spain and then we moved on to home related stuff in Toronto. George told me about the brewery walk in east Toronto he started.

George still had his soft British accent though he'd been in Canada decades. Diane's Newfoundland accent was more difficult to place. They were the sort of couple who seemed to radiate warmth for each other which then carried on radiating out to their companions. Nice company to keep. It was lovely to see these sweet, familiar faces here.

"Save the date, January 14th," said George.

I made no promises, though I would have liked to. I just honestly was not sure where I would be in January of 2020. Might as well ask me what I am doing when I get to Mars. How could I know? It was like imagining life on another planet, which is where I sensed I would soon be.

When we parted, I headed straight for my two-hour long salty bath.

Ah, the simple pleasure of reposing in a hot bath. I soaked in the relief of a journey being finished, of arriving. Arriving as a destination and permission to rest.

Still, somehow, I felt not fully arrived.

The next day, I got up bright and early to line up for my *compostela*. Arriving as ritual. The *compostela* is a certificate of completion given out at the pilgrim office, but also asserts that you have made a spiritual pilgrimage. It is written in Latin and my Latin is rusty so I take it on faith, but my understanding is you cannot have a Latin one if you have come for a purely athletic pursuit. Church's certificate, church's rules. However,

I met one woman in her late seventies who had walked from Saint-Jean-Pied-de-Port, eight hundred kilometers, and the office refused to give her one. In some miscommunication, she had been given a stamp from the office the day before and you can't have a stamp and a *compostela*—and *she* was Catholic. This seems unreasonably rules-y to me and, as you can imagine, she was not impressed either. But I digress.

The volunteer at the office gives each pilgrim a numbered ticket, like at the deli, and you return when your number is about to be called. The system is modernized with an app, which allows you to take off for a few hours and mingle with pilgrims while you await your turn. Later that afternoon I bumped into JV, who was waiting for his number to be called. I had been on the fence about whether I would attempt the walk to Finisterre or if I would take the super handy bus, which I was leaning toward, only because my feet were killing me and what I had accomplished to date seemed enough.

Also, my poles were gone.

"We will go to the sea together," he said. "No bus. No horse."

"Oh JV, I don't think so," I said.

"Ah, but it is the most beautiful walk," he said, eyes twinkling.

I tell you, that man could talk a dog off a meat wagon. In under fifteen minutes I had been convinced into walking to Finisterre, with a newly loaned set of poles and, mystery of mysteries, I was even looking forward to it. Thus agreed and committed, we planned to meet later in the main square to go for dinner.

Trickling into the square just after six in the evening, we were treated to a one-hour percussion concert by a local group of ten drummers. Drums of all shapes and sizes, colorful, smiling youth, drumming and dancing, filling the square with a joyful spirit of celebration. I spotted JV across the crowd and he had Marta with him, the Belgian songbird from the stormy San Anton evening. I was so happy to see her. We had crossed paths a couple times since but never spent any length of time together outside that first night. The two young French guys were there, too. When the German woman, Trudi, showed up, it was nearly a complete reunion of San Anton, missing only Oliver. Friends of JV, three pilgrims I had not met at all along the way, joined us, including a nine-year-old boy and his mother who had walked the whole way. Impressive. The group quickly expanded to ten and we managed to fit everyone into a large circular table in a gem of a restaurant which our German friend had recommended. It was a delightful celebration of friendship and of arriving. Arriving as shared accomplishment.

When dinner was being cleared, an eleventh person appeared, Rita. After a minute or two of conversation, we were shocked to find out that we knew each other from Ontario, if somewhat loosely. She was a good friend of Lise back home, my friend who endured my exhausting packing demo in

August, and it turned out that we had met previously at a work function. The ten of us (less the child) had just polished off the wine that came with dinner and had nothing to offer Rita, so another bottle of wine was ordered, followed on the heels by the restaurant owner blessing us with shots of his locally famous moonshine—which was delicious, but potent. We were having a grand old time, but the place was closing.

Rita said, "Hey, I'm meeting my friend Törben to hear some music. He's a Lutheran minister. Lots of fun. Want to come?"

Well, duh. Music, ministers and friends from home—of course, I want to come! Besides, how much trouble can you get into with a Lutheran minister?

As it turns out, you actually can get into a fair bit of trouble with a Lutheran minister.

As we moved from patio, to bar, back to patio, we shared some deep dive conversations about spirituality, the meaning of pilgrimage, religion, relationships, the nature of the universe, the various possibilities of God, quantum physics and the nature of time. My favorite kind of chat.

"So, who was it that spoke to you up in the mountains?" Törben asked when I shared my experience on day two in the Pyrenees.

"I know it would be easy to say God, but I am an atheist," I said. "I would say it was as if I had walked into a Divine presence, but that Divine presence was always there and already part of me. Like a curtain being lifted and for a moment you can see how things really are. No separation."

"From God?" he asked. "The Divine Presence, God, inside you and outside you?"

"She just said she is an atheist," argued Rita.

"She doesn't talk like an atheist," said Törben, laughing good-naturedly.

"I'm Buddhist, loosely anyway," I said. "Technically there is no capital G God in Buddhism. I guess to be fair there is no such thing as what we call the Self either."

"My goodness, it will be hard to know who is speaking to whom up in the mountains if now there is also no Self. No you," said Törben.

"And don't forget, no such thing as linear time," piped Rita as she ordered another glass of wine.

We closed three establishments.

Bridget and Vivi arrived the following morning, along with pouring rain. Seeing their beautiful faces filled my heart with happiness. Bridget presented me with the first of what would be two precious gifts—a shiny pink bath cap.* One for her, one for Vivi and one for me.

---

*For anyone born after 1970, a bath cap is a waterproof, often plastic, cover for the hair, secured with an elastic band.

I can imagine it might seem strange to think a bath cap precious, indeed, I can't remember the last time I even heard of a bath cap before Bridget brought up the fact that she wished she had one several towns back. I thought the whole idea was hilarious. People thought my pack list had ridiculous items—mascara, sugar scrub, a dress—but a bath cap? That takes the cake. However, it weighs nothing, you'd have to give it that. Showering was a daily delight and much appreciated in communal living, however, hair washing, not always necessary. And pilgrims with long, thick hair do have a problem once the temperature drops, as it does in Galicia, because it takes forever to dry. Inconvenient.

What was precious was not the cap itself, though the laughter we shared about the whole thing and the photo we took sporting them in front of the cathedral were priceless. The bath cap was a symbol of friendship, of sisterhood. That may sound overstated to those fortunate enough to never have been isolated by trauma, but to go from teetering on the edge of the abyss, to come all this way and finally land here and be met with love, well, it was incredible. I wouldn't have traded that bath cap and all it represented for gold.

We wandered around until lunch, taking photos at the cathedral, settling Bridget into her hotel, admiring her bathtub (you don't appreciate what you have until it's gone folks, get in your tub) and lingering over a spectacular vegetarian lunch.

Falafels. Curry. Fresh vegetables. It was a lovely, relaxing day. Another kind of arrival. Arriving together. The best kind.

After a two-hour siesta, we met again for dinner and Rita joined us. The plans we had to go to the evening Pilgrims' Mass disappeared and we all packed it in early. Saying goodbye to Bridget wasn't so bad because I was sure I would see her again in Muxía. My Celtic sister was aiming to get there for the full moon (of course). Saying goodbye to Vivi, that was hard, as I had the sense we may not see each other again. I would miss her sweetness so much. Like Bridget, she felt like a part of my very heart. In the evenings, before we turned in each night, those moments she would take to chat with her partner Rob and her daughters, the calls always full of laughter and smiles; it was beautiful. Bearing witness to all the love and warmth she had in her life, in comparison to mine, had been enormously influential and was directly related to the way I transformed my life when I returned home.

Tucked up in my spartan room later that night, in the old monastery of San Martín Pinario, I consoled my heart with a bit of writing. George and Diane from Toronto had tipped me off two days ago to the top floor in this old monastery, just outside the gate to the square, and I was able to switch out of my swanky hotel for the last night and back onto the simplicity of the pilgrim road. I was happy I had taken advice from my friend, David, back home and stayed in Santiago de Compostela longer than I had intended as it took me these entire last three days to well and truly land. I had a sense of fullness and completion now that the original journey was finished.

Tomorrow morning I would be off to Finisterre with JV. The weather promised a bit of rain, but in that moment, I was blissfully ignorant of the future, packed and ready to go.

An ending and a beginning.

Learning not to Hurry

One of my Sunday morning rituals is listening to Gil Fronsdal, a Buddhist teacher out in California, who posts his dharma talks from the Insight Meditation Center on audiodharma.org. It replaces church for me and as a bonus, can be done in bed, wearing pajamas, while drinking coffee, curled up with dogs. The best. He is a down-to-earth, humble sort of guy, with a delivery that is sweetly unpolished, and he delivers some big wisdom in a very straightforward way.

I recall one teaching he gave describing what he called the secret to life as simply "Don't hurry." It seems a paradox that when you slow down and pay attention, you feel whatever it is we call time expand, like you "get" more. He went on to explain that it's possible to be quick when necessary, without rushing, drawing from experience in his youth working in a kitchen.

The key difference lies in attention and the presence or absence of stress. When you hurry, you rush past all your moments and end up missing the whole thing because you don't stop to notice. The experience never lands. This has been coming up for me throughout the journey, with the temptation to race for beds or rushing to keep up with people or just trying to squeeze too much experience into the time I have. It is something I have always struggled with, not being able to settle into a moment, getting preoccupied with the next thing I need to do and, in doing so, robbing myself. I'm pretty sure that, for most of humans' existence, the fine ticking away of minutes and seconds was not a thing and, with the now inescapable knowledge of how many minutes have "passed," one can get a bit panicky about losing them, so we jam our minutes chock full of activity.

The way it works on the Camino is sunrise, high noon, sunset—a much gentler way to mind your days. This has a pleasantly settling effect on the nervous system.

The morning I walked into Santiago de Compostela, I was full of a quiet reverence knowing the journey was about to end and I was so grateful for it all. I purposely slowed my step to a mindful walking meditation, making a conscious effort not to hurry to the finish line and to notice everything. The birdsong up in the tree, a spider building a web in the early morning sun, the mist on the distant hills, the cows lowing in the fields. I really looked into the eyes of the smiling pilgrims as we wished each other a "Buen Camino." Each face, so beautiful. My own eyes wet with tears, I wondered if the people I met thought

I was sad, but it was just the opposite—I was brimming with gratitude and joy.

This not hurrying does not come easy to me, so with a spirit of kindness, I would make an extra effort to practice it intentionally during my remaining days on the road. The weather has been rainy and it reminds me of the one afternoon in San Anton, the old monastery ruins that housed a small hostel with no electricity or hot water. That was the night of the massive thunderstorm which created an easy intimacy as eight of us were held fast in the simple shelter by the inclement weather. With JV playing guitar and Marta singing softly, I lay tucked into a blanket in my bunk, content, enjoying the fullness and sweetness of the moment leisurely unfolding itself and having no wish to be anywhere else. Settled in body, mind and spirit. One hundred percent present.

Time means nothing in those moments.

I'd like to feel more like that, more of the time.

And as Camino fate would have it, I am heading out of town in the morning with JV, who has been walking since June, starting in Italy, so maybe I can learn something from him about not hurrying. I was glad that I lingered in Santiago to help myself land properly and part of that was to greet friends as they arrived. I did not realize how sweet it is to be a part of friends' arrivals. It is a taste of *Freudenfruede:* experiencing joy in the joy of others, contagious and delightful and the square in Santiago de Compostela is brimming with it.

This happy lingering is a first step in not rushing. But the journey is not yet complete and it is time to go now.

Time to go and not to hurry.

One Last Slap in the Face

October 16th

Turns out my friend JV was a good coach. Pre-retirement, he worked as a teacher, so he probably does it reflexively, just like I can turn into a therapist in a heartbeat. As a result of his expertise, combined with my willingness, the whole "go slowly" thing that I was hoping to adopt, happened pretty fast. I realize that sounds ridiculous, but the student was ready, the teacher appeared, and there you have it.

The first day, it poured rain for the first two hours and I was immediately drenched. Even so, I joined JV in noticing eucalyptus seeds on the ground that reminded me of tiny lotus pods and the way the light fell on the field (once the sky stopped bucketing down on us). Every now and then he would stop to appreciate a view and say how lucky we were to be here and I would pause with him and reflect with gratitude. We wandered just a little off the trail into what looked like an old mill by the ancient bridge in Ponte Maceira over the Rio Tambre.

The energy in this place was fierce and compelling, so we lingered awhile and I noticed a pentacle carved into the stone on the ground. The pagan symbol, a star inside a circle, has five points that represent earth, water, air, fire and spirit. It is a symbol of the connectedness of all. No wonder this place buzzed with energy and I would have walked right past all that if I had not been learning not to hurry. Success.

We looked up and the sky was darkening, so we started back toward the path. The rain began to pelt but we were wearing ponchos—no problem. As I looked up again, to see which way the clouds were blowing, in an attempt to forecast the remainder of our walk that day, the sky had turned a strange and ominous violet color and, shortly thereafter, began firing down hail.

"You've got to be kidding me!" I shouted at the sky.

I looked up the road and there, like a miracle in this tiny hamlet, was a bus shelter. We darted over, delighted with our luck and, from the safety of the shelter, the hail turned into a lot of fun. If we had not lingered in the pagan place by the river, we would have been fifteen minutes down the road out in the open with no shelter when the hail hit.

So, all things considered, not so bad.

That night in the albergue, I was a little dopey from the long walk in wet shoes—most unpleasant—and the general effort of this last stage, which was significantly hillier than I had anticipated. My feet were killing me. Three of us decided to do our laundry and I had the tiny, idiot-proof task of switching the clothes to the dryer. Everything goes in, you close the door and turn it on. Pretty straightforward.

Thinking I saw what was in front of me correctly, I took the clothes out of the washer, put them into what I believed to be a dryer, but was, in fact, another washer and pressed start. I immediately realized my mistake. A three Euro mistake, but I had willingly combined my things with two men's dirty underwear and smelly socks—one a total stranger—so perhaps not a mistake after all.

JV (or Alpine Jack as I started to call him), Joe the Navy Seal (the total stranger) and I washed our clothes, made dinner and went to bed, hoping only that our shoes would be dry the next day to do this all again. A modest request. There was a fair bit of snoring, not much in the way of rest and in the morning, despite newspaper stuffing and prayers to the Camino gods, we were greeted with three pairs of smelly, damp shoes.

Amazing.

I spent fifteen minutes that morning bandaging my new blisters—a present from my wet shoes—and powdering my socks and feet. I was surprised they didn't feel too bad as I stuffed them into my dank shoes.

"Just three more walks, my loves," I said to my obliging feet.

We are almost there. I feel like it's not so bad.

Well, it was bad.

That seems negative, maybe the word is difficult. Nope. That would be a lie. I'll tell you what it was. It was a little slice of hell, is what it was.

Before lunch it was just rain and wind and hills. Not terribly pleasant, but manageable. Before lunch there was the hope that the wind could change and it could all clear. "Gray skies are going to clear up, put on a happy face..."

After lunch, with twenty kilometers or more to go, hope had left the Way and the fucking monsoon arrived. A nice camaraderie of the suffering developed in the foggy bar where ten of us tried to dry off (without much success), fortify and regroup. Looking back, that's where we first encountered good-natured Jess from Australia. There was also a man, who looked to be in his early fifties, in good shape, who was on the phone trying to be sure his bag arrived at his hotel.

Bag? Hotel? Seriously, is this guy lost, or what?

"Yes, well, I understand, however, I am soaked to the bone and have another thirty kilometers to go and I want to be sure there will be dry clothes to change into," he said to person on the phone. Turned out he was talking to a bag transport company.

I'm thinking maybe buddy should have brought a day pack if he was going to ship his bag. Wouldn't he know that by now? And *another* thirty kilometers? Where was this guy going? Turns out, in case any of us were hoping to indulge in a little self-pity party, buddy was in the middle of a fifty-kilometer run.

Yes. That's why he had nothing with him. He was running through the mountains in the pouring rain, I assume of his own free will, as I saw no one chasing him with a gun.

When he hung up, I got a chance to speak to him.

"Pretty horrid day for a run, no?" I said.

"Well, better than heat," he said. "Once you get used to it, the rain is actually quite refreshing."

"Hmm," I said.

What I thought was: *A refreshing rain? Oh, come on...*

"I don't mind the rain, I just want to be sure I'll have dry clothes to get into after a hot shower," he said.

"Fair enough," I said.

It must be said that, truly, I do not understand what drives people like this. I admire them, but I do not understand them. (Did I mention the monsoon?)

Other than my personal feelings of inadequacy brought on by the drenched running man, it was a nice half hour and included hot things like lentil soup and tea, but the last twenty kilometers were not going to walk themselves, so we all put our cold, wet things back on and pushed ever onward and upward—*Ultreia et Suseia,* as the saying goes. Alpine Jack commented that in the war, the soldiers often had to go out in terrible weather in wet things, horribly uncomfortable conditions and, while I did appreciate this, I thought *OK, but we are not IN a war, Jack.*

Thirty kilometers in the soaking rain and gusting wind. Maybe for three kilometers it was not raining, but that's it. In no other circumstance that I can think of, would I be out wandering around in this kind of weather. None. I am wearing an enormous red poncho, which is now wet inside and out with rain and sweat and it is whipping, with feeling, I might add, around me and my pack, which is still getting wet despite being covered with the poncho. If it hadn't been so expensive, I would tear the damn thing off and throw it on the ground.

To keep the water from soaking my face, I walked with my head down, looking only at the ground in front of me, so if there was a view on this day, I missed it. No longer important to avoid puddles, much like the cow patties, because it is now all a puddle, and it is all shit, and I am soaked to the bone. Much of the time we are walking on a road with cars flying past, which feels dangerous and more than a little stupid.

The evening before this debacle ensued, having not really enjoyed being wet and in pain, I made an inquiry to a nice little Casa Rural which was around the twenty-kilometer mark instead of the thirty-two, or whatever the target was we had discussed. Having walked for so many weeks now, I knew my body well enough to determine I was not going to be up for a thirty kilometer walk in bad weather, so I made an escape plan. It was perfect. Stopping there would make the following days a little longer, but it was a sensible plan. I didn't mention the plan to my walking mate, which was a little weird, but I think I sorted it out just in case. I would still try to go the distance, but if things were not good, I wouldn't be stuck. Very sensible back pocket plan.

I think it is quite clear at this point that things, without a shadow of doubt, were not good. Not even in the *neighborhood* of good. So obviously when I reached the Casa Rural, I stayed. Right?

You would think so.

The village appears, Alpine Jack is ahead of me and powering past it, which is totally fair because I have not mentioned that I may stay here and his intention had always been to continue another twelve or so kilometers. I don't expect him to read my mind. He doesn't know that I feel like getting hit by one of these cars whizzing past might be acceptable if it means I can at last stop walking, for the love of God. I think about shouting over the wind to get his attention to let him know I am finished, but I don't have the energy. I think about just stopping and let him figure it out when he sees that I have disappeared. But I had decided to walk into Finisterre with my friend and I still want to do that, despite my feet falling off and me running out of time. I hesitate and turn back to gaze over my shoulder.

I was remembering what I read about the sweet couple who run the Casa Rural, the fire in the cozy bar downstairs, private rooms with sheets and towels. I imagined how it would feel, at that moment, to walk into a warm, welcoming place with a fire, take a hot shower, sit by the fire in dry clothes, maybe sipping a port. I feel all that, deeply feel it in my exhausted flesh, do a double take and I keep walking.

Unbelievable, but true.

At this point, my feet are seizing up and I am stumbling more than walking. I have been drenched from ten minutes after lunch. Misery. My body is giving me all the information I need to inform me that we are well past done here. And yet for some mysterious reason, I do not turn around.

Twenty yards after me aborting my plan to take care of myself, the wind and rain pick up ferociously and come at me sideways, nearly blowing me into the road. It keeps driving and driving and driving. I have the distinct sense I am getting a personal message from Mother Nature, in fact, I believe she has just slapped me in the face to make a point crystal clear. Out of love of course. All Camino lessons are born of love.

What exactly is going on here? Is it that I do not want to be beaten by Alpine Jack and the Navy Seal?

No. I don't think that is the reason because I am not particularly competitive. In fact, one nearly completed walk across Spain notwithstanding, I would normally describe myself as a bit lazy.

As I continued to get blasted about, it began to dawn on me; my body was screaming STOP and I refused to listen, refused to take care of myself. Why?

That storm certainly got my attention and the osteopath's sentence from many weeks ago drifted back as the wind buffeted me, "It is not the point of the Camino to suffer." When tired, rest. Fairly simple point. Compassion for self as well as others—an old lesson. We do not need to earn comfort and care.

I promised myself that I would stop at the next opportunity, which unfortunately turned out to be eight kilometers away. This doesn't sound like much if your legs aren't broken and you're not walking in a monsoon, up and down hills in every direction so the rain gets a good chance at soaking every inch of you, but it did in fact feel like an impossible distance.

I notice that Jack turns around periodically to see that I am not in a ditch (very kind), but eventually he stops in the road to wait for me. I explained how hobbled I had become and let him know I would be staying at the next stop, my way of telling him he can go on ahead, but as I said, he is very kind and refused to leave me stumbling around the hills, despite me trying, sincerely, to dispatch him.

As we approach the top of what I think must be the final hill, which turns out not to be the final hill—classic— struggling to catch my breath, with the wind and the rain blowing from all directions, it occurs to me this would be a beautiful walk under different conditions, especially this exact spot. It reminds me of Ireland with the bright green hills, the cows and the rain. Leaning over on my walking sticks as I gaze back over the sodden, pastoral landscape we have traversed, with labored breathing, I look at JV who is gazing into the distance and he turns his head slowly—dare I say, theatrically—to look back at me with a mischievous grin.

Don't do it Jack, don't even *think* about mentioning the beautiful view.

"Listen. I am not feeling lucky, or blessed and I am not having a good time here, Jack," I spit, as I get the sense he's going to do it again. He's going to count the damn blessings. He's going to stop and be amazed at all the beauty, this time just to annoy me.

He makes a sweeping gesture with his arm alerting me to the brilliant, soggy landscape and turns back to me and cracks up laughing.

"Oh, for fuck's sake, Jack!" I shout over the wind and then we are both laughing.

The whole sodden thing is just ridiculous.

The albergue, when it mercifully emerged, was heaven on earth. There was heat, hot water, cold beer, a bottom bunk with a real duvet. There was also a friendly manager and three other smart people who wanted to share a cab with me the following morning to get us to the bus stop which would bring us to Cee—the town we were meant to walk to.

The weather did not improve overnight, it got worse if that was possible, poured the entire day and flooded roads. That next morning, I was riding shotgun with the manager's husband who had volunteered to take us to the bus as all the cabs were booked for the morning *(what a surprise)*. The defrost didn't seem to be keeping up with our steamy breath, so I was wiping the inside of the windshield and side window with a sock (that had once been a tub plug) so he could sort of see along the foggy, drenched and winding roads. We did not see many pilgrims walking, but we saw a handful. The four of us were quite pleased to be in the car, let me tell you.

No regret there. Zippo. Nada.

I was relieved to see my friend Jack arrive in the albergue in Cee that afternoon. He was drenched and frozen, but smiling as always. When he came in, I was happily tucked up on the couch, under a blanket with Jess, who had also been on the bus, We sipped our hot tea and listened, as he regaled us with his stories of roads that had turned into rivers and other miseries that I was thankfully not a part of because I was here, enjoying the day and being kind to myself.

Lesson learned, Mother Nature, lesson learned.

.

Arriving Part Two.

Finisterre

We celebrated JV's arrival in Cee with a decadent, sumptuous meal—our last time cooking together. It had always been me cooking and he did the washing up, which suited me just fine (I despise washing up). When I asked him if he cooked at home, he said his wife was Ministry of Food and he was Ministry of Nature. He tended the garden and she turned out fantastic meals. You know, you do this and I'll do that, and we will each respect the other's dominions and leave each other in peace. Smart.

"There is one rule in my garden," said JV seriously.

"Do tell," I said, thinking a garden rule from JV must be something.

"No shoes," he said, wagging his finger. "No boots. Barefoot only."

I asked him why he had this rule, expecting that it was some complicated horticultural thing.

"Just for fun," he said, smiling. "To touch the earth."

Rules to encourage joy and fun. What a great idea.

Dinner was fantastic—mushrooms in red wine, garlic, butter and cream, baguette, cheese, a bottle of Rioja tinto. JV contributed some chocolate for dessert and treated us to more guitar playing after we wrapped up. I slept deeply that night, grateful for the day of rest, for the company of friends, for the food and the music, for my dry shoes and for the fun fact that tomorrow was going to be the last day of walking. For real this time.

Mother of mercy, it is finally here.

We emerged from the woods south of Sardiñeiro de Abaixo and were greeted by a sweeping view of the ocean and the first glimpse of Cape Finisterre, jutting out into the water. Magnificent. Whooping with abandon and delight, I launched into a joyous, "I see the finish line" dance. If there ever was a dancing moment, surely it is when you see the finish line of a nearly nine-hundred-kilometer walk. A time for celebration, a time for a grateful dance of joy. Even the sun was dancing.

How I have missed you, Sun.

The weather mostly held that morning and thanks to the skillful albergue owners, we all had dry shoes—even JV who had been soaked to the bone. It was a short walk, maybe twelve kilometers or so. We hopped onto the beach for the last kilometer, sat down and got rid of our shoes, laughing with delight. Ah, sand underfoot and in between my toes, bliss.

JV scoured the beach for a proper shell. He was honouring the old way of pilgrims and collecting his shell at the completion of pilgrimage, not the beginning, and he seemed to be looking for something particular. I went to commune with the sea.

Before I wandered away, I touched his arm and said, "You were right, my friend."

"About what?" he said.

"Walking here. This was the only way to finish the journey. The best way. Even with the monsoon," I admitted.

"Especially with the monsoon," he laughed.

JV went off along the empty beach to find his shell and I walked into the gentle surf, just enough for the salt water to kiss my exhausted feet. This arrival, walking out of the woods, across the sand and into the ocean, this was profound in a way that Santiago wasn't for me.

"Thank you," I whispered into the sea and up to the sky, grateful, my eyes full of happy tears. "Thank you for everything."

I searched my pockets and found the rock I picked up on our way out of Santiago, on which I had written her name and set it down.

"Keep her safe. Watch over her. Help her remember."

If I couldn't reach Bea, I was certain this energy that accompanied me all along the Way, the energy I felt coming up through my feet on the beach, that limitless power could reach her. I was sure of it.

I stood, rooted, feeling supported by the Universe, feeling that I was never alone and that I had been helped the entire way by guides in disguise and unseen forces of love—just like this ocean kiss. Surrounded, cradled and sheltered by a cloak of love. I was overcome with an enormous gratitude and thought how funny it was when people remarked how brave I was to walk alone. I was never alone!

I left a message in the sand for all that had helped me get here, through all the trials and all the blessings, such deep gratitude for my mended heart, "*Gracias por todo.*"

Eventually, after indulging in some serious dallying and lingering along the beach, we picked our way to our hostel, bumping into several people we knew along the way, including those friends from Australia with the bug bites and Joe the Navy Seal. We made our way along the last three kilometers to the zero marker at the lighthouse on the cape, Cabo Finisterre, end of the world. I didn't bring any object to burn—an old tradition, now illegal yet clearly still practiced. It felt unnecessary to me because it seemed the whole journey I had been steadily burning about a ton of negative karma and I felt entirely cleansed.

We sat separately for a while on the rocks as the ocean roared and splashed below. I thought of my sister Nancy, who didn't materialize along the Way as I hoped she would and imagined how life might have been different for her if she'd had the opportunity to walk the Camino, if she'd had the inclination and support to do so. I thought about my nearly lost daughter. This is the place where we let go of everything—at the end of the earth. What have I learned about this letting go?

Ultimately, I didn't do this walk thinking it would restore my relationship with Bea; I knew that was not within my power. I did it to save my own heart stopping from the pain of being very nearly exiled from her life. That in itself was a miracle—I could live awhile with that. And I had to accept that life may just continue this way; I could always return for more medicine.

Yes, acceptance was the way—not resignation, which carries the hopeless feeling of defeat. Acceptance brings with it a sense of peace. Acknowledging this is how things are now, I must find a way to adapt to it—just for now, not for eternity. There is room for hope in acceptance and that feels healthy, because I will not give up hope.

This place that looks like the finish line, is actually a doorway and it is good to pause before passing. Feeling the rocks underneath me, feeling the ocean air on my skin, I closed my eyes and inhaled; long and deep. *Strong back, Soft front,* a meditation from Joan Halifax was with me. I sat that way for several minutes, drawing upon all that had happened to strengthen my spine over these last weeks so I could keep my newly mended heart open as I contemplated an ending and a beginning.

JV decided to hike up to the top for the view, which is apparently stunning, but I wouldn't know because done is done and I was done. Zero kilometers, no more walking for me. While waiting for JV to return, I took the opportunity to have a rest in Bar O'Refuxio where I met an American and an Irishman who regaled me with the most beautiful Camino love story.

They had met a young man early in their journey from Scotland who had set out to walk when his grandparents had died. The grandparents had this crazy romantic story about separately walking out of the house or the jail or wherever each was stuck the day the war ended and had walked, full of gratitude for their lives, along the Camino Francés, right here to Finisterre. As Camino luck would have it, Scottish Grandpa meets lovely French lass along the Way, they fall instantly in love and, tragically, get separated.

Miraculously, they met again, each reaching Finisterre at the same time. They were not going to make that mistake again so got married immediately, of course. These are the days before Tinder and Plenty of Fish where there is always the promise of an upgrade one swipe away. Anyway, they lived a charmed love story, made a wonderful, rich life together, had kids and grandkids. But then she died. And you know this guy is not getting left twice, so he dies shortly thereafter.

The grandson adored his grandparents and, clearly, their deaths left him bereft. In an act of love, he decided to honor them by walking the Camino in his grandfather's kilt. Never changed out of it, according to the storytellers.

Guess what happens.

You know how it is said we attract things to us with the energy we put out around ourselves? Well, this guy is doing a walk full of love, soaked through with love for his departed grandparents, who were themselves full of love. Scottish guy, full of love, surrounded by love, on a road soaked in love, sporting a kilt. You know what happens, yes?

That's right, early in the walk, the grandson meets a French girl, he falls madly in love with her and...

She goes home.

"You're joking!" I say, all but shouting and nearly falling off my perch.

"Tragic," says the Irish pilgrim. "Brokenhearted, so he was."

"Inconsolable," says the American.

I'm crushed. God help me, I'm a hopeless romantic.

"This is a terrible story!" I say by way of protest.

"Aye, but 'tis not over, lass," he said.

All was not lost because, in this modern-day love story, it's Facebook to the rescue. They got in touch and she was coming to meet him here at Cape Finisterre when he arrived, which was today. They thought they might see him again as they assumed he'd ask her to marry him at sunset.

Of course he would. What fool would not see that, unbeknownst to him, he is wearing a magic kilt and has just been handed the love of his life by his dead grandparents.

You will have to stay in suspense, as will I, as this kilted romantic never did materialize, but the two storytellers joined JV, me and Joe the Navy seal for a glorious, breathtaking sunset behind the bar. We were joined by a family of wild goats roaming the rocks below, bah-ing or mah-ing or whatever it is that goats do while they totally ignored the sunset. It was a magical moment, a perfectly peaceful, wouldn't-change-a-thing sort of moment.

I chose to believe we didn't see the kilted grandson because he was on the beach with the French girl and that she believed in Camino magic and said "Yes" and that their grandparents' spirits were dancing beside them on the sand.

There is simply no help for me. No help at all.

The next day, we made for Muxía. JV and Joe on foot and me on the bus. Done is done, my friends.

Done is done.

Arriving Part Three.
Muxía

If Finisterre was the end of the physical journey for me, arriving in wild Muxía was the end of the spirit journey. There was magic here. The energy was beckoning, wrapping itself around me, getting into my flesh and bones—something powerful and familiar. I loved it.

Bridget had stayed in Muxía an extra night waiting for me to arrive so we could have a proper farewell. All along the Way, she would stop and channel poems as they came to her—I've never seen anything like it. She said that she herself did not write them, but it was more like she was the vehicle or vessel for their birth. However they came to her, she could effortlessly paint spirit with her words.

We got caught up over a much-needed *café con leche*, realizing how little time remained before she had to leave to catch her flight. We cashed out and meandered through the sprawling open air market, through the winding streets of the tiny town and up along the sea wall to the point where The Virgin of the Boat church sits. It appears to be close enough to the roaring sea to set sail. The raw wild intensity of the sea was mesmerizing. We walked down onto the rocks to feel the ocean for a bit, but I was drawn back up the hill, past the rock sculpture, to where the boulders were strewn about.

Muxía is intriguing. There is a deep, strong feminine energy, the energy of birthing and burying. Some of the stones even look like reclining women. This is a place of pagan energy, a place of creation, but of destruction, too. The wind was fierce, maybe a storm on its way.

"The wind changes the weather," I remember the old nun, the Guardian of the Bells, saying as she stopped mid-conversation and looked up to the sky more than a month ago in Zabaldika. She looked to the sky not like someone checking for signs of the actual weather, but like a mystic or a soothsayer, like she was listening to something none of us could hear. The wind changes weather, changes fortune. We are meant to move, to allow the river to take us up with it, not to resist or stay rigid and stagnant. The wind brings change.

Have I been here before? I found myself wondering as we walked amongst the huge rocks, allowing my fingers to trail along the cold stone and damp moss. *Have we been here before?*

I was convinced in that moment that I was, in fact, a druid or witch of some sort in the past, that Bridget and Vivi were also, and that we had been in this place together long ago mixing up potions and calling to the sea. Had I been enjoying too much Outlander on Netflix? Perhaps way too much? Yes, perhaps. And we *had* been singing "The Skye Boat Song" just a few days back as we walked through the woods. Nevertheless, it all felt very familiar.

After an hour or so lingering on the stones at the top of the hill, listening to the ocean crash on the shore, we returned to the patio to await Bridget's bus to Santiago. We were comparing stamps in our *credencials* again, as we had done in Samos. This time I noticed the beautiful red stamp from the iron smith just before the wine fountain in Irache.

"Hey, this was a great place," I said, pointing to the stamp. "I wanted to bring so many things home with me and didn't even buy a piece of jewelry because I didn't want to add any weight. How dumb was that."

Bridget smiled and pulled up her shell necklace from the smith to show me.

"That is perfect," I said, touching the pendant. "I thought I would find something in Santiago, but nothing spoke to me the same, so I didn't bother getting anything."

"Oh," she said, smiling, "this must be for you. I knew I was getting it for someone."

She reached into her bag and after some rummaging, my dear friend retrieved another shell pendant necklace from the smith and handed it to me; an amulet to take home and a tangible reminder that I did not imagine all this wonder. I had a feeling I would need that as I returned to the ordinary world.

Oof. My heart. First the bath cap and now this. I've been tucked away in the dark for a long, long time and these simple tokens of affection are more important than I can explain.

Just then, I heard a familiar voice. "Colleen?"

"Frankie!" I jumped up to hug my old friend, surprised and delighted by the sight of him.

"Amiga!"

What are the chances? We hadn't seen each other since the tiny village of Reliegos before León. We had a quick chat, arranged to catch up later that day and he made off for his hostel, which turned out to be the same as mine. Bridget's bus arrived not too long after Frankie departed. Another goodbye to tug at my heart. But it is only farewell, until we meet again.

Friendship, seeing and being seen, has been such an enormous part of the healing that has taken place on this journey. It astounds me really, how deeply I had hidden myself. We can't expect people to see us if we are hiding and we need to be seen to heal. It is an important part of the process. Faith, trust and courage, my borrowed mantra, is what's required to step out of the shadows.

"As you start to walk out on the way, the way appears." Rumi

It was a great couple of days catching up with old friends and absorbing all the magic in this place. The next morning, I roamed the point again, up by the Virgin of the Boat, this time with JV, who had arrived, as always, on foot.

Frankie reappeared just before I went to bed on that final night, so I stayed up a little longer to chat in the communal kitchen. His unusual hair cut had started growing back, the shorn sides filing in. Just before I had met him, he had stopped in a hair salon in Burgos, the shining city, and asked for a trim. What he asked for was a little off the sides, but perhaps with some miscommunication, Spanish to English, it turned into shaved sides and long floppy hair on the top, secured with gel. He told us about the incident at dinner when we met Queenie way back in Hornillos.

"I didn't bring any gel with me. Who brings gel on the Camino? What am I supposed to do with this when I wash the gel out?" he had said as he ran his fingers through his coif, or tried to.

Frankie was the sort of person who seemed to like to know the history of a place while he was in it. I had met many people like that along the way, not uncommon, especially on a journey such as this. I, on the other hand, prefer to absorb the whole essence of a thing, the gestalt perhaps, and that experience gets lost for me if I try to follow too many details. Just different ways to approach things. Obviously, I sometimes miss important points this way.

While we were talking, Frankie pointed me to information on the wall that clearly outlined the pagan history of Muxía, the rocks, some other fun facts it might have been interesting to know had I looked at the wall. At some point during the conversation, we talked about our time in Santiago and he mentioned the renovations at the Cathedral, how disappointing it was there was no *botafumeiro* this year but wasn't it great you could still get in to hug the apostle and...

"Wait, what?!" my ears perked up.

"You know, St James. Santiago?" He was perplexed that I was perplexed. "The apostle..."

"Wait," I said. "So, I was in the cathedral, in this huge line up, thought I was going into the museum, never bothered to ask anyone and, when we finally got inside the archway, the guy in front of me bends over and hugs this, this head..." I said, my ignorance all dawning on me at once, "and I was like, whatever rocks your boat. Oh my god. What a ding-dong."

"You didn't know that was St James?" he said, laughing. "How did you not know that?"

Apparently, everyone knows this and, even if you didn't, everyone at some point prior to their visit to the cathedral reads the guidebook, right? Nope. One guidebook, three apps and zero information. And whose fault is that?

Shaking my head, "So that casket everyone was kneeling in front of..."

He nods his head slowly, smiling.

We say goodnight and goodbye for now. In the morning, I would board a bus with JV, his first since leaving Italy. We are bound once again to Santiago de Compostela, a first stop on our routes in different directions, returning, each in our own ways, to life after the Camino. An important arrival itself, perhaps the most important—how we arrive back in our lives.

I finished my pilgrimage, not with all my dreams come true, but restored, returned to myself; what a gift it was simply to belong to myself once again and to be alive in the world. My spirit, once withered, now restored and able to hold both sorrow and joy, as we all must. The pain that had me in tatters, though still painful, would not crush me again.

HOMECOMING

Instructions on Returning

Meeting My Spirit

If we listen closely, there will be instructions given on how to return. These guiding arrows are happening all along the way, but some lessons are a bit more, shall we say, pointed.

Arriving happened not only at the end, but everyday there was an arrival, all different, all the same. It could be said that we arrived in each moment over the forty days; some held more significance than others, some were the attention-getting kind that stop you in your tracks. There was the time in the Meseta, when I met myself walking and stepped back into my strength. Glorious. And earlier, alone in the Pyrenees when Grace scooped me up on day two and gave me a Get out of Jail Free card, saving me from my delusion of separateness. Astonishing. And there were others.

Those times were nothing short of transcendent.

The one that informed how I would return home, happened in a little town called Barbadelo, just past Sarria, where I was introduced to my spirit. Kind of the Universe to give me the soft stuff first and the difficult stuff at the end, once I was mended enough to be ready for it.

Unexpectedly, sweet Vivi was the bridge. Vivi, the person who showed me all the sweet joy of connection that I was missing. Vivi, the serendipitous friend who, just by being herself, showed me how empty I had allowed my life to become while I waited—barely existing—waited for my daughter to return, waited for my stolen life and stolen voice to return.

It is said that the first third of the Camino — the Basque Country and the Rioja — is where you face your physical challenge, the Meseta is where you grapple with your mind and Galicia is where you find the spiritual challenge. Although I didn't buy into that neat little order, I guess what unfolded shouldn't have surprised me. Funny, I was taking 'spiritual' as a rather existential sort of thing, expecting a gentle, meditative sort of wander through the rolling green Galician hills. Also, I thought I had been given my allotted big "Spiritual Experience" back in the Pyrenees, so to be fair, I thought that bit was complete.

Well, it wasn't.

I can still see the horrid gray room outside of the tiny town of Barbadelo, close to that all important spot where you know there are only 100 kilometers to get to Santiago. It was the worst sleeping situation on the entire Camino, in some metal shed someone had converted, just barely, to house six sets of bunk beds. No heat. No nearby food. Not even remotely clean. And the peculiar, officious owner who followed us around like an ill-tempered border collie, insisted I take a top bunk, even though a bottom bunk was free, even after I tried to explain how sore my feet were. I ended up on the top bunk over Vivi, who offered me hers, but her feet were not much better, so I refused. The nearness of my dear friends was the only saving grace that evening.

I'm not sure what started my reflection, other than insomnia providing an opportunity. Thinking back, I'm not even sure I would call it reflection. Perhaps it started as reflection, but it ended up as an altered state of consciousness. As the clock ticked away into the darkness, I could sense a building energy of anxiety, which slowly transformed into something I would call dread. I lay staring at the ceiling, under a pile of clothes to ward off the chill and tried to calm myself with breathing. It wasn't helping. Sleeping with music is not something I normally do, but I decided to try that to quiet my spirit, putting on a playlist full of Debussy, Puccini, Handel and Arvo Pärt. Soft. Comforting.

If I tell you a voice told me to do something, you will deduce that after walking all that way, I had finally, at long last, gone entirely mad, but I don't know how else to explain it. Perhaps was it my own voice? The one that had been stolen by the king of the crickets years ago.* If you are hearing from the deep seat of your own soul, have you just heard your true voice? And if that voice had been silenced for years by abuse, by trauma, what might that be like?

It was like seeing a ghost.

In another moment of Grace, the music turned into a raft and I was being supported by it, ferried across the night—disembodied, floating. And with my body held and my mind pacified, my spirit was able to communicate with me.

Over several hours that sleepless night, my spirit introduced herself and, though kind, she is all business—a bit like a loving, but very serious parent who is outlining a sorely needed course correction. That is when I knew that what was going to happen next, what I would need to bring about, would be like tossing a grenade into the middle of my life. I wasn't happy, sure, but to walk out of my built life into nothing? At fifty-two years old? What a terrifying contemplation.

The other option to just go back to life as I knew it, after all the hard work, would be like throwing away all the gifts and blessings that had been bestowed. To be honest, I was more than a little nervous about what would happen if I ignored this little talking to.

---

* From The Little Mute Boy, Federico Garcia Lorca, about a stolen voice

There is no unknowing what is known, no unseeing what is seen.

Something was waiting to be born, but I needed to die to my old life first. Everything that didn't fit had to go. I needed to make space for Joy, for love, for purpose and passion. If you are lucky, you can make these changes one at a time. I knew that would not work for me because I had everything all tangled up in one great big knot.

On a raft of music, I allowed myself to be carried through the long night. I was able to hear my spirit and I knew I could not return to my life as I had constructed it; there was no question. It simply didn't fit or serve my spirit. In fact, what I had allowed my life to deteriorate into—and I hold only myself responsible for this—was for certain beneath the dignity of my spirit. Believe me, I tried to bargain. I was gently instructed to let go and let the raft of the music continue to carry me until whatever was happening—and it sounds strange, but something was happening—until it was complete. In the end, I knew what needed to be done.

When I got back to Toronto and looked around me, I knew all I would miss, but I also knew it was impossible to stay. When you are living someone else's life, there is no room for the one that was meant for you to emerge. Exposed, thanks to Vivi, to the potential fullness of a life lived with love, I now knew that I had to make some room.

If I were to have any chance of lasting joy, I had to mourn what I had lost and move forward, alone. I had to let go of everything, even waiting for my beloved daughter. She was an adult and she knew I loved her. I would have to trust her to find her way back, in her own time and in her own way.

The Cross

"Ours is not a caravan of despair!"

Rumi

Joseph, my first Camino guide at Beilari, had an exercise at the family table before dinner while he was surreptitiously training us to become pilgrims. He asked people to give their pilgrimage a title or a theme in two or three words, much better than asking people "why" they came. The reason why is too big and often too personal; many people aren't sure why they came until weeks later and the people who are sure, like me, are not sure they want to share it.

I offered mine, *"Restoring Joy."*

Over the whole course of the journey, woven through all the trials, there were abundant moments and interactions that all built one upon the other to mend my spirit and create capacity for Joy to be restored, but there were a few pivotal points, such as crossing the Pyrenees, walking along the Meseta, at the Iron Cross and lying awake in Barbadelo, where some major shifts happened, brought about simply by an increasing awareness of the divine presence of Love underlying all things and a realization of no separation. The kind of moments that take your breath away.

The one I have yet to describe, was Cruz de Ferro, or the Iron Cross. It is the highest elevation along the Way and approaching it, it seems to buzz with energy. This is the much-anticipated place people often deposit a rock as a symbol of whatever burden they carry and, in the words of Elsa from Frozen, "Let it go, let it go!" Strangely enough, and surprising to me, I did leave a song. I had nothing physical to leave, because I could find nothing physical which truly symbolized my loss, and I came to the Cross empty-handed, trusting I would know what to do once I got there.

As I approached the massive mound of rocks, the simple metal cross way atop what looked like a telephone pole, the air felt increasingly charged. All these rocks represented the prayers, hopes, wishes and gratitude of pilgrims, each one held in someone's hand before they set it down. Each stone suffused with emotion—some kind of alchemy is happening here.

It is impossible to stand in this space and not know in your bones that you are not alone in your sorrow. Our sorrows have different names, shapes, sizes and stories, but they, the sorrows themselves, are familiar with each other. There in front of me, stood a physical symbol of our collective sorrow and of what goes hand in hand with sorrow—the tenderness of love.

I walked slowly forward, watching as the wind battered the pilgrims' plastic ponchos and as I walked, I felt a song bubbling up to the surface, all on its own.

Yes, of course.

Passing dear JV, who was sitting on a bench in solitary, tearful reflection, I stood back by the trees, alone, my voice finding its way. I sang the song into the energy of the space, felt it be carried by the wind and the tears brushed from my cheeks. A song of love, but not a love song, that represented all I had lost and all my heart longed for. A lullaby, the one I had sung to Bea every night as I tucked her into bed so many years ago, in her little room decorated like an enchanted forest. I could see her in front of me, feel her in my arms. "I Will" by the Beatles.

Who knows how long I've loved you
You know I love you still
Will I wait a lonely lifetime
If you want me to, I will...

Listening to the words freshly as they left my lips, I thought how interesting that all along it had been a prophecy I had been singing to my sweet child, just like the Briar Rose book given to her by her grandmother. It made me wonder if there isn't some part of us that knows what our future holds and proceeds, nevertheless. Leaving the lullaby and all it represented at the cross, I did indeed feel freed of a clutching to what I had hoped for and cleared space for what might be. Bittersweet, but certainly better.

"And when at last I find you, your song will fill the air."

A mother's memory of love, of holding my daughter in my arms, of reading books together, of how earnest she was even as a toddler, of laughing at all manner of silliness, of afternoon tea in the kitchen, of the sweet music of her voice, of road trip adventures and summers on Cape Cod, of going to all her Improv shows and field hockey games, of sharing the story of life's unfolding, of being there when she needed me, of sitting across from her in a cafe and seeing love reflected back from her eyes, of my daughter not becoming a stranger. It all came rushing back to me.

A mother's memory of her daughter.

A mother's memory of being a mother.

A mother sending a lullaby into the wind.

Of course, the grief bubbled up along with the rest. Regret for not being able to protect her from all that happened to split her in two. After years of trying, I had to admit, I could not do anything if she could not hear me. But I could still love her. I could send it out on the wind. And I still had time to save myself, so she had a mother to return to someday, if, as my Camino daughter Hannah said, "she will remember you, maybe she just needs time."

There is no power greater than Love.

Love remains.

I remain.

I have seen it all along the Way: Love lifting us up, carrying us, connecting us. I saw it from the moment I met Rosemary in Joseph's kitchen, I was drenched with it in the Pyrenees on the second day and I walked into an energy field of it at the Cross. Anything that is not Love, is not worth thinking about.

Love is the answer, Love is the path and Love is the medicine.

Time has no dominion over Love.

I can see that here in front of me in this mound of rocks.

All. This. Love.

Instead of a gaping hole in my heart, I had room in my heart. Instead of a heart withered by bitterness, I felt life's breath filling its chambers.

As I strode over the slate mountain through the rain to el Acebo, I felt free. My heart was at peace. And though I knew it would continue to require tending, the mortal wound was mended.

. . .

I probably should say something about the trauma and how that was impacted, so I will say that the person who set out on this journey, ostracized, full of pain and despair, is barely recognizable to me. I am amazed, humbled, healed and grateful. All along the way, I just became more and more of who I already am, not different, just more of me; taller, stronger, happier. Imagine, to meet yourself, in the middle of your life, after you have, for so long, forgotten yourself—what a gift.

This river of strangers, no longer strangers, created a river of love with their energy and brought me back to life. For me, walking the Camino was learning to step into the river with both feet. To commit to the ebb and flow, with all the possibilities and all the potential calamities—the full catastrophe, as Jon Kabat Zinn and Zorba the Greek have said.

The cure for trauma is to live. It is found in the present, not the past and is as simple as stepping over a threshold (which is not truly simple). It is to climb out of the story and join the present moment.

Just this step. Just this breath.

Everything is right here.

Can you imagine a more perfect place to learn how to live again, than on a pilgrimage full of people who are full of love, all walking each other home? Thinking back to the container of love created by the Italian volunteers in Ermita San Nicolas, the warm welcome at the door, the hosts delighted at the arrival of each pilgrim, the sweet cook ministering to us with his wild humor as well as the meal he created with love, the older man with whom I shared no language who bear hugged me at least three times during my stay. The nurse who carried his own first aid kit to help others along the way, tending blisters, including mine, on the stone floor by headlamp. In encounters like these all along the way, a pendulation between walking and landing, bit by bit, my heart started to heal. Even tiny exchanges became small stitches in the heart.

Change isn't easy, but if we do not change, we do not grow. Faith and trust get you so far, but the courage part, that seems to come at the end of the journey.

The courage to make your life your own.

It continues to amaze me, years later, the way I was met by whatever that energy is in the Universe on just the second day, full of benevolence and love, a feeling of pure spirit moving through me, reminding me that I am loved and I belong here and that no matter how dark it gets, that love will always be there, right beside me.

Love is the answer to...well, everything.

I will never forget it.

Ultreia et suseia!

EPILOGUE

Epilogue
Gathering in the Glade

*"Everything you love is very likely to be lost, but in the end,
love will return in a different way."*

Franz Kafka

Scene: The first of November, 2024, Samhain in the old Celtic calendar, when the veil between the Living and the Dead is said to be thinnest. We are sitting in the kitchen in a house in Hamilton, Ontario on a very mixed weather day. Looking out the window, sunny, cloudy, stormy, rainy, back to sunny...basically, everything. A raft of make-up on the table in front of me.

"Sit still," said Bea as she applied yet more bronzer to my cheeks.

"OK, but I'm not used to this," I said.

She stood back and looked at me, smiling, "Mum, so beautiful. You are glowing!"

I felt awkward. I was not used to be tended to in this way, not used to make-up application in just the right light and not used to my daughter being, well, a daughter. And I would hazard a guess that the whole thing was pretty unusual for her, too. This kind of sweet intimacy that had once been our normal connection, had been dormant for many years. We were pulling from history here, both in genuine good faith. Turns out that love returning can be a bit bumpy.

There was knock on the door.

Libby, the very old beagle, now deaf, did not budge from the couch.

"I'll get it," said Bea.

November 1st 2024—five years almost to the date of my return from Camino and we are in a very different place.

. . .

Late November 2019, Yarmouth, Massachusetts...

"If you could just sign here. This indicates you understand you can't store flammable or explosive materials in the unit. No food. And you can't live in it," said the clerk with a straight face.

"You have to tell people that?" I asked, shocked.

"You'd be surprised," she said. "It's cheap rent."

Concerning in a few ways. I signed, got the key to my new storage locker, cube C108, and went back out into the late, cold and grey November afternoon to meet my future, in Yarmouth, Massachusetts.

If years ago, someone had told me I would ever have a storage locker, I would have laughed, especially after forty days on a Camino living out of a backpack. However, these weren't extra things. These were *all* my things. The downsized reality of my material possessions now fit into a five by ten-foot cube.

Joseph Campbell said, "You must be able to let go of the life you had planned in order to live the life that is waiting for you." Well, boy, did I ever let go. I don't recommend changing everything at once if you can avoid it. I couldn't avoid it, so it was an uncomfortable couple of months, let me tell you. But now that I was firmly reconnected with my spirit, wearing my old life, even for a day, was like putting on someone else's pants.

. . .

As I loaded up my new storage locker, I thought back to the Camino meeting in Toronto earlier that month, when I was standing at the threshold to this new life.

I was giving a backpack demonstration for new pilgrims, "Yes, bring good socks, no you won't need the sugar scrub," and I had bumped into David, whom I knew from a handful of Camino meetings and walks.

"Hey," he said, looking at the contents of my pack on the table as he was passing. "Is that lipstick? You're kidding!"

"Don't judge," I said laughing. *Am I flirting with this man?*

At that time, I had already ended an eight-year relationship— something quite difficult—and had begun initial plans to move back to Boston. I felt like a bunch of confetti tossed in the air, somewhere between flight and crashed back to earth; scattered yet free.

David and I talked a couple times that day, just briefly, mostly about Camino stuff.

"People say the hardest part of the Camino is when you come back," he said. "Are you finding that?"

"Well, I basically threw a grenade into my life, so I'd say, yeah, I agree with that."

I told him about the ended relationship, the upcoming move, not being sure what was next but trusting the spirit that guided me.

"It would appear that I am in *between lives*," I said, theatrically.

He nodded like he understood—I didn't know then just how much he understood.

"When do you leave for Boston," he asked.

"The weekend before Thanksgiving," I said.

"Don't go," he said.

He shifted his weight from side to side, uncomfortable, like he also was surprised about what just came out of his mouth and quickly said a few other things like, of course you need to go, and another thing or two I can't remember, functionally dismissing the "Don't go" as some pleasantry and, yet, it just hung there in the air, like a big yellow arrow.

I was surprised and stumbled in response. It didn't make any sense, but I could feel the energy there and, of course, I was leaving, so the whole notion was ridiculous.

It was not time. Everything in the right time.

Here's a shout out to Canadian healthcare, because, even dispatched as I was, having already filled up the Yarmouth storage locker and now existing in that liminal space between lives on Cape Cod, awaiting the arrival of my 89-year-old mother who was no longer managing in the retirement home and, without a clue of the global pandemic that was on our doorstep, at which time I would be isolated with my mum for many months, I needed to return to Toronto for medical appointments.

This included, ironically, a vaccine.

. . .

It was a snowy January night and I shivered as I waited outside the Spadina subway station back in Toronto. My new friend, David, from the Camino group (the one who advised me to stay longer in Santiago, the one who helped me get documents for repatriation to the Pilgrim House, poked fun at my lipstick, then told me not to leave—that David), had heard I was back in town and offered, well, to this day I am not sure what he offered, but to meet and catch up at least, which is funny as we didn't really know each other well enough to catch up; a few Toronto Camino meetings and bumping into each other at John Brierley's talk notwithstanding. Anyway, for some reason, I agreed.

"There you are," said David as he rounded the corner with a smile on his face. "I was just at the other exit to see if you were there. It's so good to see you!"

We hugged hello, through big puffy winter jackets and he felt so familiar, even though he wasn't—at least not in this lifetime.

"There's a good pub down along Bloor. Sound OK?" he asked.

"Sounds great," I said. When we arrived, a table for two in the window magically vacated and we spent a lovely hour there swapping Camino tales, the windows steaming up beside us, cold outside and warm inside, watching the snow fall. Turned out they were about to broadcast a big wrestling match to the TV beside our table, so we thought it best to change venues.

"Hey, do you have *A Hug for the Apostle*?" he asked.

"Is that the classic Camino book by Laurie Dennett?" I asked.

"That's the one. Canada's Doyenne of the Camino," he said with a smile.

"I do not," I said, recalling my shocking lack of information in Santiago and my utter confusion at the man hugging the stone head. This didn't seem the moment to share the impressive extent of my ignorance.

"Well, I have two and I want to give you one. I'm just around the corner," he said.

It was still early so off we went through the snow to his apartment, which truly was just around the corner.

"How about a nightcap," said David. "I think it is a Scotch night," he said looking at the snow falling outside the bay window.

I relayed him the story of the search throughout Scotland for a scotch I could even remotely enjoy (it was not successful) and that it was unlikely that I would like the scotch he offered me, so perhaps just a drop to be social.

"I take that as a challenge," he said and produced a decanter and two whiskey tumblers.

I expected to politely nurse the few drops of what was offered and head home.

It was delicious, as was the conversation.

One glass led to another, one topic led to another, all woven together with commonalities, moments of mutual recognition, another book was loaned based on some confessed sadness about my relationship with my daughter. It felt like we had known each other forever. All sweet and pure and friendly, but the evening extended far past either party's intention and, next thing you know, it was nearly two in the morning and the subway was about to stop for the night.

The rest of the weekend, I was in a bit of a fog, wondering, was I on a date without knowing it? That would be just like me. When I described it to friends, they all agreed, it sounded very much like a date.

"So, he invited you out," said Lise.

"Yes, but just for a pint and to catch up," I said.

"Uh huh," said Nora. "A six hour catch up? With someone you barely know?"

"That wasn't intended," I said. "He had a book to lend me and it just kind of...continued."

"Continued to his apartment," said Lise with a raised brow.

"Well, that is where the book was and we were avoiding the wrestling match," I said.

"Right. A book you didn't ask for...did he have art to show you as well?" said Nora. Now they were just enjoying themselves.

"And you actually didn't know you were on a date?" Lise said. "You really are out of practice."

"But I'm sure it didn't start as a date," I said bewildered.

Even though it was perfectly platonic, there was just something about it, couldn't put my finger on it. *No, I am sure it was perfectly normal.*

Safely back on Cape Cod within a week, I settled in to get as much writing as I could before my mother moved in the following month. Four days later, I received a message from David that he had found the companion book to the one he lent me, *The Tao of Pooh* by Benjamin Hoff.

"What a coincidence," I said and I sent him a section I was reading at that moment.

"How can you get very far, If you don't know Who you are? How can you do what you ought, If you don't know What You've Got? And if you don't know Which to Do of all the things in front of you, Then what you'll have when you are through Is just a mess without a clue Of all the best that can come true If you know What and Which and Who."

It seemed to get right to the heart of my scattered post-Camino attention and I wanted to convey my gratitude for the thoughtful loan. The friendship that I assumed would fade away with a border in between, continued, in part, because there was room. Because I had created room.

Something was being born.

It went from philosophy, to writing, to concerns about children. We shared music, ideas about food, mysticism, magic, everything Camino, stargazing, astrology and relationships. Our connection was a gift, especially in the isolation that followed during the 2020 lockdown. The calls started out weeks apart, usually starting with some invented reason and then evolved into an hour or more of great conversation. They were such fun, full of laughter and sweetness. We even had movie nights, watching the same streaming movie on the laptop while remaining on the phone.

"Ok, we both press play on one. Ready?" asked David.

"Ready," I said.

"OK, three, two, one," said David.

"Wait, *on* one?" I asked.

"Oh, *come on*," he laughed.

It was impossible to begin at the same second, much to each other's amusement.

Let's face it, by this point, it wasn't really about the movies.

I was enjoying all of it, enjoying his wonderful company and didn't notice exactly when the calls started hitting the two-hour mark, becoming almost daily at one point, and getting a little flirtatious. Just playfully, but in a way that left me looking forward to the next call, the next silly message, all of which eventually led me to penning a small stack of love letters.

We all did kooky things during the pandemic, mine was a stack of unsent love letters, fountain pen on fine paper, procured from a lovingly curated shop in Truro, Massachusetts. Thankfully, my brother stopped by on just the right day, saw what I was doing at the kitchen table and saved me from myself.

"Colleen! You can't send those!" said Marty, visibly shocked.

"Why not?" I said.

"All these?" he said as he picked up the stack, counting them. "Twenty-two?! What the hell are you doing?"

He started reading aloud the titles I had written on the back flaps, "New Moon, Chapin Beach, River Behavior, A Confession...a confession? Oh my God."

He was apoplectic.

"Well, obviously I am not going to send them all at once. Just one a week," I said as I reached for the stamps.

"This man will think you are bonkers. No. I'm not letting you do this to yourself," he said as he pocketed the stamps and walked away, mumbling, "She's cracked."

"Who's hacked?" piped my mother from her easy chair. At eighty-nine, was deaf as a haddock.

"Cracked! Your daughter is cracked," said Marty.

"Couldn't you just bake a bunch of bread like everyone else," he said as he left with my stamps.

"I don't bake," I said, following him to the door.

"Well, you should take it up," he said. "You'll thank me for this one day."

It was just long enough for my good sense to return.

. . .

Though the most important result of the Camino was the return of me to myself and, though my heart's desire was (and always would be) the return of my daughter, I did want a whole life, full of love, reminiscent of what I saw in Vivi's phone calls. By healing my heart enough to keep it open without falling apart and by creating space in my life, there was a way for love to return to me, not in the form I was expecting, but love sometimes returns another way, as Franz Kafka said.

. . .

Real change takes time. Healing takes time. It had been a rollercoaster ride from the end of my Camino in 2019 to a beautiful fall day in 2024. It was all worth it.

The knock at the door was our lovely neighbour, Tim.

"Your limo awaits," he said with a flourish. "Right this way."

We stepped out into the early November sunshine, down the steps and into the back of his SUV where we found two glasses of champagne waiting for us.

"Nice touch," I said, surprised.

"Red dress," said Tim. "Nice choice."

"The color of love," I said. "Searched all over Spain for this."

It was only a few blocks to the woods, so we thought about walking, but good sense prevailed and we took this time to really appreciate all that had transpired in the last five years to bring about this moment. We had planned the day carefully, turning it into a bit of a Camino with different stages.

Tim let us out and scooted ahead with Libby, the ancient beagle, who was wearing a red bow, and disappeared around a bend to join Bea and the others who had already gathered.

We paused at the entrance to the glade and looked at each other.

Another threshold—a momentous one.

"Ready?" asked David, beaming at me, resplendent in his Scottish clan's tartan kilt.

"So ready," I said, taking his hand.

We walked up the winding path and, as we turned a corner, there they all were, standing in the sunny autumn glade, smiling and cheering, a place transformed by love and joy. People from both our families looking back at us and dozens of our friends and community, here together in this sacred space; the space made holy by love.

A portal in the woods.

It was one of the most beautiful and unexpected moments of my life.

Bea joined us as we made our way into the center, a carpet of fallen leaves of red and gold at our feet. Beautiful Bea. My daughter. After David and I decided to get married that January (on the anniversary of the Scotch date), I had asked her, tentatively, how she would feel about standing up for her mother at the wedding. She had been returning to relationship in fits and starts and I didn't want to scare her away, but she agreed enthusiastically and agreed to come over from Paris, where she was now living.

Hannah predicted it back in Burgos—Bea found her way back, following the thread of connection that remained. My heart was overflowing.

Our Camino wedding went on all day.

We celebrated together in the sacred glade. We wandered down to the church hall to join our musician friends for a ceilidh and, finally, to the local diner for tapas and 1930's jazz. We celebrated the next day, too.

Bea returned to her life in Paris.

It is hard, when you feel that you have lost so much time with someone you love, not to feel greedy. The only thing that keeps you from acting on that greed is love. Love is open and free (this can be turned into a mantra as needed). We cannot have what is here when we keep looking in the rearview mirror.

That stack of love letters remains, mostly unopened, wrapped in orange tissue paper, tucked safely away in my sunny studio in our home—the sanctuary David and I created together. Every once in a while, I look at them, thank my brother for his wisdom and tuck them back away.

David keeps asking for them.

Everything in time.

A few weeks after the celebration, a friend sent us some photos she took of the wedding in the glade. There were some of the woods surrounding us, one of us walking up the path and one that took my breath.

"Hello Mum," I said, smiling at the photo. "I knew you'd come. That's why we had it on the first of November."

There she was, a little blue orb floating over us as we held hands in the center of the glade, surrounded by love. Just like the grandparent spirits celebrating with the pilgrim couple we heard about in Finisterre, my mother was with us that day, despite her death two years earlier; one of our unseen honored guests.

As long as there is Love, everything is possible.

ACKNOWLEDGMENTS

This book baby could not have been born without David "O'Duncan," my sweetheart, my husband, my gift from the Universe and my long-suffering in-house editor—you have my gratitude as well as my heart. To my mum, Nancy, who had endless enthusiasm for my stories and insisted on having the blog entries read to her as soon as they came out. To my sister, Maureen, who provided at least a decade of gentle, unfailingly hopeful counsel in an impossible situation.

To JC, who loaned me my mantra – *Faith, Trust and Courage* and prepared my heart before I set out (along with the help of porch poets and philosophers throughout the summer of 2019). Rosemary, who gently waited as I found my way across the bridge. To my dear Camino sisters, Armorel and Tové, and all the beautiful humans I walked amongst, too many to name. To our Camino community in Canada, especially the Toronto community who prepared me to go and the Hamilton community who continues to sustain me years later.

To Laurie Dennett, Rebekah Scott, and the other pioneers who continue to remind us of the importance of the Traditional Way. Most of the healing that happened, happened in community. We must protect this.

To Libby, the ancient beagle, my whole heart. Thank you for picking me up in the dark, nudging me with your cold, wet nose.

To Kim Narenkivicius — pilgrim, *anam cara,* and publisher of *Stone Boat Editions* — who sparkles with magic and makes the world more beautiful anywhere she turns her attention.

To the artists: Mary, our local visionary and bold community builder who created her own community and brought about this community book launch. Debbie Finn, who created a gorgeous cover, intuiting the journey, who inspires us all finding Joy in the dark. Illustrator Caillin Kowalczyk, who joined the party to create an otherworldly map worthy of the journey.

Community....we do better together.

To the three High Priestesses in the sacred circle, you know who you are. Blessings.

For the trees.

For the quiet and determined guidance of the ancestors.

And, for my beloved daughter—wow, how you impress me with your guts, your fortitude, your beautiful big heart, your capacity for Joy and peace and compassion. Thank you for trusting me, for remembering, for returning. I love you more than you know. Go have an amazing life!

My gratitude and love to you all.

ABOUT THE AUTHOR

Colleen is a writer, occupational therapist, pilgrim guide and the human of a very devoted beagle. She and her husband David, live in Hamilton, Ontario and are coordinators of their local *Canadian Company of Pilgrims* chapter, or as they call themselves, *Communitas Co-pilots*. She is also a member of the Boston Chapter of *American Pilgrims on the Camino*, an editor of the national Camino newsletter, *Pilgrim Footprints*, a pilgrim, and very dear to her heart, she is an hospitalera and a hospitalero trainer. She maintains a private clinical practice in Hamilton, Ontario and continues to strive to bring awareness to the extreme grief and mental health issues related to familial alienation. She began a trauma-informed, semi-supported Camino program, *Let's Walk Home,* in 2024 and continues work in researching the therapeutic effects of pilgrimage after difficult life experiences.

Learn more at colleenotoole.com

ARTISTS

COVER PAINTING BY DEBORAH FINN

Debbie Finn is a self-taught artist based in Hamilton, Ontario, whose bold, expressive acrylic paintings are created primarily with a palette knife. She was commissioned to create the cover artwork for Colleen's *Restoring Joy,* capturing the spirit of the story through her vibrant style. Her work has been shown in group exhibitions across Ontario and is held in private collections throughout Canada. @debbiefinn6

BACK ALLEY GALLERY, MARY FLYNN

Mary Flynn is the founder of Back Alley Gallery, a garage-turned-studio in Hamilton, Ontario. The space has grown into a vibrant hub for local artists, offering rotating exhibits and welcoming workshops that foster creativity, connection, and community. She hosted an opening celebration for *Restoring Joy,* featuring the group show *The Way Within.* @backalley.gallery

ILLUSTRATIONS BY CAILLIN KOWALCZYK

Caillin Kowalczyk is an artist and illustrator from Hamilton, Ontario, whose work explores the interplay of art, architecture, and place. His series *I'm so lost and I live just around the corner* draws inspiration from local urban landscapes. Influenced by graffiti, comics, and nature, he also works as a goldsmith specializing in custom design. @caillin.lovesick

Stone Boat Editions is an independent publisher moored in the mountain village of Rabanal del Camino, along the ancient route of the Camino Francés. Devoted to the spirit of pilgrimage, we curate work that speaks to the soul of the journey.

Through our books and curated anthologies, we gather the voices of writers, artists, and seekers from around the world, offering stories from *The Way* — a record of this moment on the Camino, and an invitation to all who feel called to set out on the long, beautiful, and mysterious road to Santiago. *Ultreia!*

thestoneboat.com

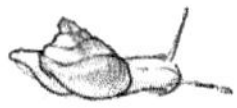

www.ingramcontent.com/pod-product-compliance
Lightning Source LLC
Chambersburg PA
CBHW030819090426
42737CB00009B/797